Loads and Roads in Scotland and Beyond

Places referred to in the text

Loads and Roads in Scotland and Beyond

Land Transport over 6000 Years

Edited by

ALEXANDER FENTON

and

GEOFFREY STELL

A Scottish History and Culture Paperback

JOHN DONALD PUBLISHERS LTD
EDINBURGH

ISBN 0 85976 107 X

Exclusive distribution in the United States of America and Canada by Humanities Press Inc., Atlantic Highlands, NJ 07716, USA.

Phototypeset, printed and bound by Bell and Bain, Ltd., Glasgow, Scotland.

Introduction

The papers brought together in this book were originally presented as a one-day conference organised by Geoffrey Stell for the Society of Antiquaries of Scotland. Ted Ruddock's survey has been complemented by a detailed case-study of the Old Bridge at Bridge of Earn. A paper on the distribution of carts and wagons has also been added, since it not only extends perspectives, but also looks at distribution patterns on maps. This is something that John Coles also refers to for the prehistoric period. Geoffrey Barrow's paper represents a revised version of the Presidential Address that he delivered to the Scottish History Society in December 1973.

Over the 6000 years that the papers cover, there are many gaps that remain to be filled. Nevertheless the links between prehistory, the Roman and medieval periods, and the more recent past, come out strongly. These chapters bring the story of land transport in Scotland up to the 18th century, taking account of timeless traditions that long survived changes in means of transport. Historians, geographers, students of place-names and material culture, engineers, archaeologists, all who read these pages closely, as they deserve, will find themselves left with a far livelier and more realistic impression of the ways in which our ancestors overcame difficulties of transport and communication. They will find themselves crossing rivers with Dougal the Ferryman of 600 years ago, or walking along the oldest road in the world, the Sweet Track in the Somerset Levels, built with amazing skill and ingenuity 6000 years back in time. They will cease to think that all the people of the past lived primitive lives; many did, but prehistory, like later ages, had its leaders too. 'Civilisation' is not unique to the century we live in.

Contributors

Professor Geoffrey Barrow, Department of Scottish History, University of Edinburgh.

Professor John Coles, Department of Archaeology, University of Cambridge.

Dr Alexander Fenton, National Museum of Antiquities of Scotland.

Geoffrey Hay, Royal Commission on the Ancient and Historical Monuments of Scotland.

Gordon Maxwell, Royal Commission on the Ancient and Historical Monuments of Scotland.

Ted Ruddock, Department of Architecture, University of Edinburgh.

Geoffrey Stell, Royal Commission on the Ancient and Historical Monuments of Scotland.

Contents

Prehistoric Roads and Trackways in Britain:

Problems and Possibilities

J.M. Coles

The subject of prehistoric roads and trackways is one that allows, even persuades, the prehistorian to indulge in conjecture unencumbered by the need to pay attention to observable evidence. Prehistoric roads and trackways existed in the past, probably in great abundance, variety and complexity, but they hardly exist today in clearly recognisable forms, and they tend therefore to be totally neglected by archaeologists. Before these problems are examined, however, a few comments will be made about ancient roads in general, as these may help us to understand what questions we might legitimately ask about prehistoric travel, transport and communication in Britain.

If we look at various ancient societies in the Old and New Worlds, one general observation can be made: the character and extent of a country's roads provide a mirror of its organisation, its central control or lack of it, the regularity of links between its main units, and its general need for cohesion. The Romans, for example, probably the greatest road builders of antiquity, linked their provinces with a series of graded and drained roadways that still survive to interest modern roadbuilders; the Romans depended upon these clearly-marked roads not only for commercial and political traffic, but also for symbolic reasons in demonstrating the efficiency, the control and the power of the Empire and its constituent members. If we take another example, well over 500 years ago the inhabitants of Peru constructed not only architecture of massive character but also a vast series of roads in mountainous areas of the Andes in order to unite the scattered hamlets that owed tribute to the Inca capital of Cuzco; these roads were made for foot traffic, for pack animals and for sledges, and they too provided a demonstration of the territorial power of the ruling state.

The Romans of course had wheeled vehicles and they therefore made their roads accordingly, wide and well-drained and at a relatively low or shallow gradient. The Inca had no wheeled vehicles as such, and their roads could therefore be narrower and steeper. The Ancient British also had no wheeled vehicles until late in their prehistory, and although finds may turn up somewhere and sometime, at the moment this lack of vehicles in Britain is matched by the fact that there are no known prehistoric roads in Britain that were clearly made for such traffic.

Both the Romans and the Inca were well organised societies, and they may have exceeded the needs of prehistoric British or European communities to create and maintain roads and paths. I emphasise the word needs, the needs of prehistoric communities to build roads, because there can be no doubt that the prehistoric societies of Europe had the technical skill to lay out roads, had the manpower to build them, and had sufficient tenure of the land to make it worthwhile to maintain traditional routes. All of these we can document, but the surviving evidence is nowhere equivalent to the Wimpey-like engineering works of the Romans, or the Inca.

Instead, for closer analogy, we must look elsewhere, to areas where central states did not exist, where there was no single controlling unit of government, where there was no master plan for the nation, no bureaucratic organisation able to create a policy, order its completion, maintain its existence, as well as create problems and delays, ignore good advice, and generally make a mess of things sometimes, as we know the Romans did, and as perhaps the Inca did. And a useful model in our attempts to understand the problems of British prehistoric roads and tracks is the native Indian societies in Canada; here, we have the benefit not only of the archaeological record but also of historic documentation at the time of European penetration.

The largest political unit in Canada at the time of European settlement was the tribe, too small in numbers, too self-contained, and often too unsettled to demand or need purposefully-built roadways for maintaining communication and travel between areas. There were no wheeled vehicles among the Indian tribes, but this did not prevent them using other methods of transport, and although oxen and horses for draught animals were not present as indigenous animals, travel and communication were prolific in eastern America, with materials and ideas moved freely over long distances by direct or indirect methods (fig. 1). There was no

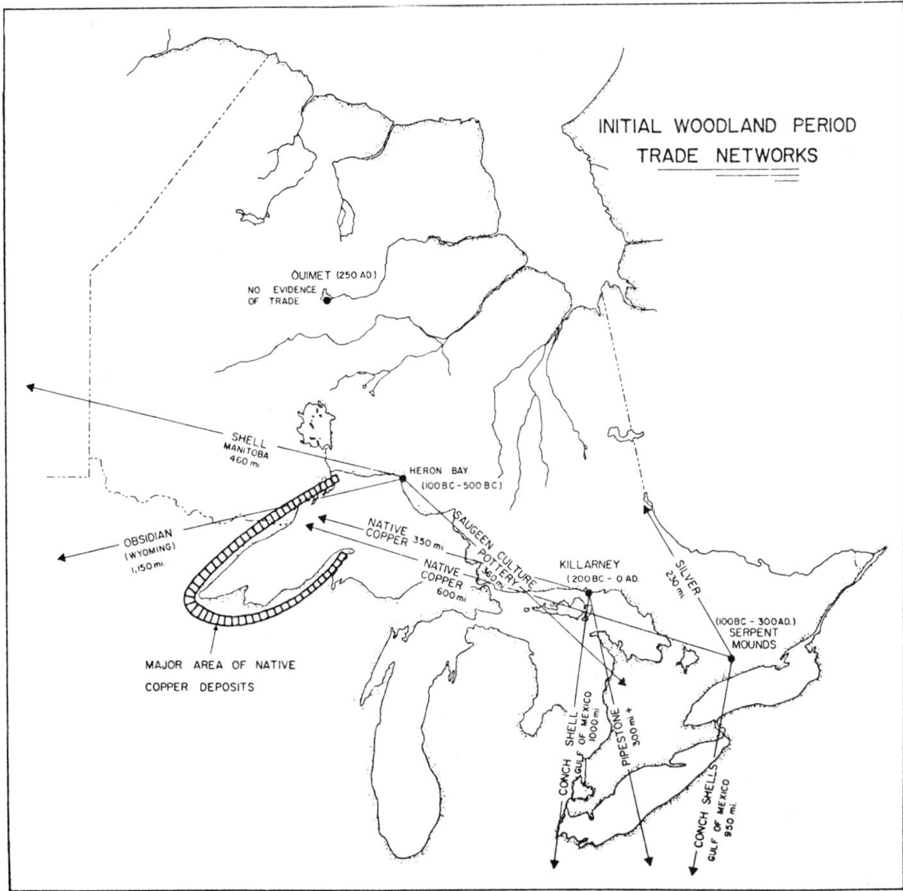

Fig. 1. Distribution map of the Great Lakes region in Ontario, Canada. St James Bay and part of Hudson Bay are at the top of the map. The trade networks of the Initial Woodland period, *c*. 1000 B.C.–A.D. 1000, were extensive, and yet there were no established and maintained road systems.

central state, although very late in its prehistory the Iroquois confederacy offered the opportunities of political alliances and wider exchanges; these did not last long with the incursions of Europeans.

Yet even with widespread trade in earlier times, and with some political alliances, and with a long tradition of land tenure and exploitation, throughout the entire region of pioneering Canada (Upper and Lower) there was not a single mile of roadway before the Europeans arrived, nothing but a series of narrow paths or trails through forest, plain or upland, beside rapids and canyons, sometimes linking valleys but in no way providing anything resembling a planned network. Often these paths were overgrown, hardly different from animal trails, and, importantly, often the human groups who wished to move would use the animal paths, or stream beds, as much as any human footpath. Dense undergrowth was avoided, rocky ground too as it damaged the feet and shoes; instead, the uplands were the favoured ground for walking, and where these were treeless, or where the grasslands were abundant, no paths at all were necessary; man could walk where he wished. Where a tribe was quite populous, with well-established villages, then a few paths would gradually become well-used, even maintained, linking one community with another, but there were no bridges across intervening streams, no wooded or stone-laid road surfaces, no straight lines or artificial gradients, no rhyme or reason except the easiest wild and natural routes between areas of occupation.

Although I would not argue that these examples provide any close guide to the identification of prehistoric routes and roads in Britain, they do I think point to some of the possibilities as well as the problems we face. Even if we accept that the elucidation of a country's routes and roads can throw light on the nature of the societies which established and maintained them, we must also admit that many of the parts and segments of the communication systems will never be recognisable or identifiable. Prehistorians have three opportunities to distinguish the nature of ancient routes and roads, namely, the absolute documentation of actual built roads and tracks, the observation of present day natural geological formations which may have eased travel, and the conjectural restoration of ancient routes of prehistoric time. These three different archaeological possibilities can be briefly described in ascending order of quality as:

a) Evidence for contacts and communication, entirely conjectural, based upon distributions of artifacts and raw materials.

b) Evidence for routes, natural geological formations, of ridges, plains, coastlines or valleys, physically suitable for human movement along them, and sometimes yielding archaeological material in suggestive locations.

c) Evidence for roads and tracks, artificial or 'made roads', established and maintained by known early groups to guarantee safe passages.

Distribution networks

Turning now to Britain and western Europe, we can look at the first of these sources, the suggestive information of distribution maps. These maps are produced by prehistorians in their efforts to explain how things are related, how industries worked, how sites and objects were placed in the landscape, and how societies managed to organise themselves and to divide up the land economically and politically. Archaeological maps are often covered by spots, and occasionally conjectural lines may be drawn joining the spots (fig. 2), as if to suggest 'connections', or lines may be drawn around groups of spots (fig. 3), as if to suggest lack of 'connections' or 'territoriality'; more archaeologists tend to leave the spots alone, as if they explain themselves, and occasionally some spots will be enlarged, to suggest that these are 'central places'. In no case, to my knowledge, has any effort been made to show how such spots, of whatever size, were linked physically, by deliberate humanly-made

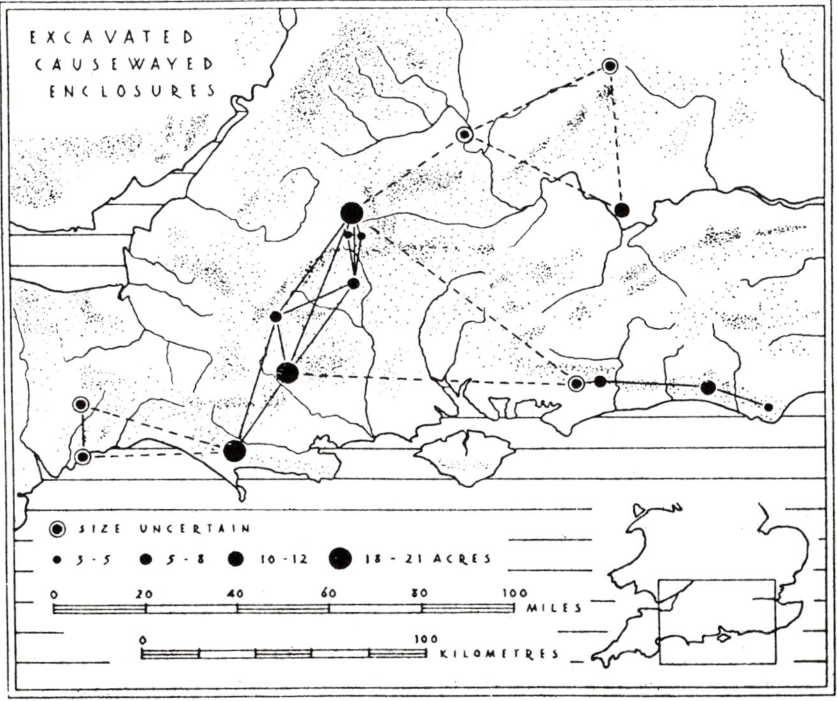

Fig. 2. Map of south-central England with the major Neolithic causewayed enclosures marked, and an attempt to show distances and linkage between them.

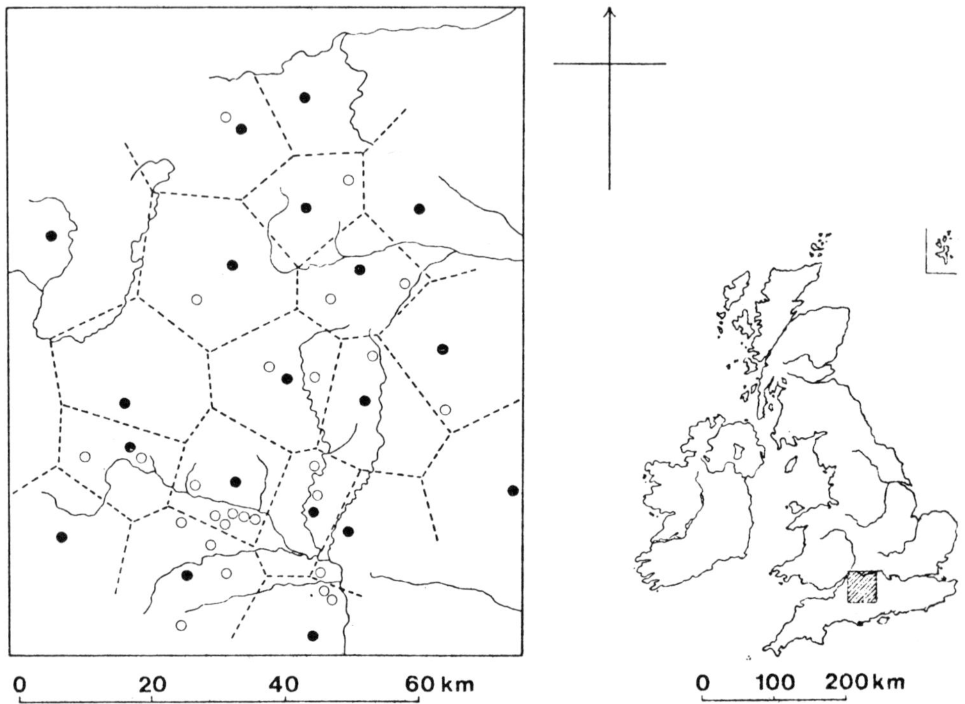

Fig. 3. Map of west-central England with hillforts in Wiltshire shown. The open circles mark hillforts in use in the sixth century B.C., and the solid circles mark those of the first century B.C. The hypothetical territorial boundaries are marked by the dashed lines.

roads or paths or trails. The tendency of archaeologists to put large spots on small maps often totally masks even the gross estimate of distances between spots, and discourages any real thought on the movement of materials or human groups. Hardly ever are the spots on archaeological maps put on a detailed physical background which attempts to represent the ancient environmental conditions and which would at once suggest potential lines of communication, or difficulties of communication, or even the opportunities for archaeological discoveries of missing pieces. How can we begin to talk of, for example, major and minor markets of the British Iron Age (fig. 4) when we know nothing about the roads, the ease or difficulty of communication, what vehicles or transport might have been used, what animals if any were used, how long were the journeys, which settlements lay on the routes, what were the

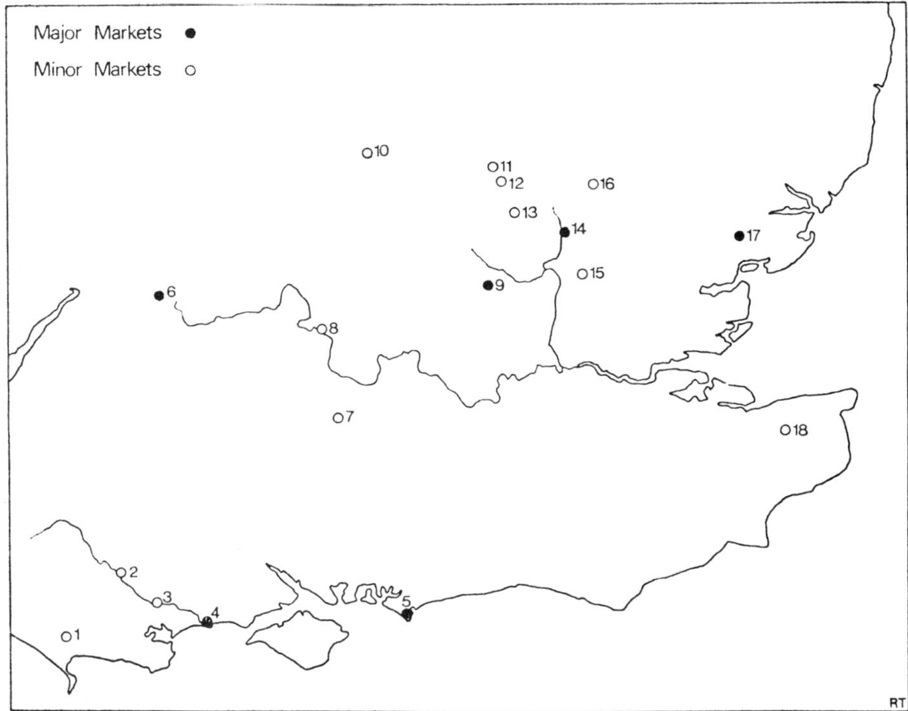

Fig. 4. Distribution of major and minor market centres in south-eastern England, first century B.C.—first century A.D. In the absence of indications of landscape features, the distances and connections between markets are difficult to appreciate.

weights of possible cargoes or loads, and why were such journeys necessary? This example seems to illustrate all of the problems about communication that archaeologists consistently ignore.

A road is by definition a fixed and well-defined way, paved or prepared to stand up to the wear of regular traffic, people, animals, carts or caravans. Roads today are such a dominant part of life that we may think they were always present in some form or other. But they were not. Apart from a very brief and important episode of road building under the Romans, Britain and western Europe had no roads of a fixed, permanent and maintained character until well into the second millennium A.D., that is, only three or four centuries ago. There are a few exceptions, to which I will return shortly.

But we cannot of course accept that, because there were no fixed roads ('made roads' is a useful term), there were no movements in ancient times, no communication, no travel. The distribution maps of related groups of artifacts, and particularly those analytically characterised to a precise source, such as stone axes, suggest links of one sort or another, and therefore movement. Although many of these maps refer to the Neolithic 'stone axe trade', there is interesting evidence from the Mesolithic period as well. The acquisition of a large variety of raw materials from the rocks and minerals of central eastern Scotland, for example, was apparently a regular part of the seasonally variable life of the occupants of the settlement at Morton, Fife, and indicates the existence of traditional pathways from the coast into the Howe of Fife, the estuary of the Tay, the Ochil and perhaps the Sidlaw Hills (fig. 5).

Archaeologists are rightly concerned with the reasons why artifacts are distributed around the landscape, how they came to be placed, or be found, over such wide areas, and prehistorians assume that the agencies and vehicles, in the non-literal sense, existed for movement and were efficiently employed. But the precise details of organisation and management of methods of communication and

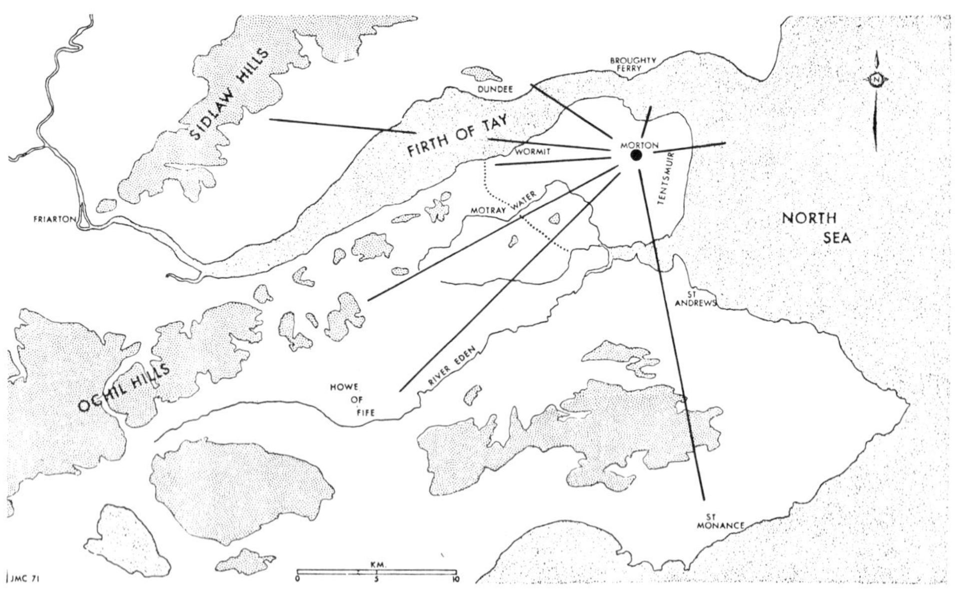

Fig. 5. Map of east-central Scotland with the Mesolithic site of Morton, Fife, shown. The lines extend to areas around Morton that were probably visited by the Mesolithic group in its seasonal rounds, when rocks and minerals were collected for working into the stone tools found at Morton.

traffic are not yet available to us. Early man, whether a Mesolithic hunter, a Neolithic herdsman, a Bronze Age farmer, an Iron Age merchant, a Dark Age missionary, or even a post-conquest tinker, had to make his own way, and choose the best of possible ways, seasonally variable no doubt, in order to get to his destination. Problems must have existed over location as well, and doubtless many landmarks were devised and perhaps established to mark the most economical way. We know very little about directional indicators in ancient times, especially if we exclude, I hope, the astro-archaeological bodies of evidence; there may have been distance marks, arrowlike alignments of stones or wooden posts for the traveller, or carved figures on stone or wood as direction indicators, and there would have been plenty of natural guides, such as the sun and stars, mountain peaks and the like. These would have been suitable for both land and sea travel.

Although our immediate concern is land transport, we cannot neglect the fact that traffic in prehistoric times would have relied to a great extent on water transport. The island character of Britain and Ireland necessitated regular crossings of North Sea, Irish Sea or Channel, although we as yet lack knowledge of any craft suitable for these waters. Logboats, rafts and plank-built boats from the Bronze Age would have allowed traffic in estuaries and rivers, thereby avoiding the problem of negotiating dense woodland and marshy valleys. Distributions of artifacts suggest the former existence of landing places, fords and even riverside docks from which land transport would take over. The wide distribution of Rhum bloodstone and Arran pitchstone, for example, on mainland Scottish Neolithic sites demonstrates the existence of some regular transport by water as well as its subsequent carriage across the land. I think it unlikely that we can attempt to understand either land travel or sea travel in isolation from each other.

The problems of archaeological distribution maps are great, but they remain a fruitful source of suggestions, and possibilities, about prehistoric travel and transport; when allied to observable natural land routes, they can combine to produce clear guides to the general identification of preferred passages in ancient times.

Routes

No discussion of ancient land traffic can avoid mention of the famous Ways of southern England, the Icknield Way–Ridgeway route, the Pilgrims' Way–Harroway route, the South Downs Ridgeway or even the Jurassic Way. That these great natural ridges existed in prehistoric times is not in dispute; what is less certain is the period, or periods, when they came into regular use as routes.

They would have provided a series of upland walkways which might have been attractive to early man in his search for ways by which to ensure easy movement between settlements and natural resources. Some of these Ways have been identified as of prehistoric origin because there are many monuments such as burial mounds scattered along their routes. But with increased knowledge of the distribution of prehistoric monuments, it would now seem that the allegedly significant concentrations on the Ways are more diffuse and generalised, and there is not much now to support the evidence for direct and purposeful traffic along some of these Ways in prehistoric times; the Ridgeway and the Pilgrims' Way are examples of natural routes which may have been established in the Neolithic, but the evidence is now slight indeed. And perhaps the same is true for the Jurassic Way, an enormously long and broad geological formation extending from Lincoln in the east to Glastonbury in the west; the width of the Way is such that it can hardly be called a route, and its distribution of prehistoric monuments and other artifacts can be explained in various ways which reduce the evidence for actual movement of traffic along the Way.

Better evidence exists for the Icknield Way which provided a route from the Thames up to the Wash; it is marked by a series of Neolithic and Bronze Age monuments along its course, but the distribution of these monuments and other artifacts such as imported stone axes is now more clearly seen as a generalised spread along the area of the Way rather than the particularised close association often postulated (fig. 6). The Way was wide and broad, and there is no evidence in prehistoric times of a fixed carriageway or even walkway. Instead the traveller would pick, within the whole width of the ridge, the best, firmest, hardest and driest way, and where wheeled vehicles were used in later times, their furrows and ruts show the random nature of the actual passage along the ridge. The Icknield Way is generally considered to be the oldest traditional route in Britain. This may still be so, and it is certainly one of the longest-lived passageways. But there is another candidate for the oldest road, as we shall see.

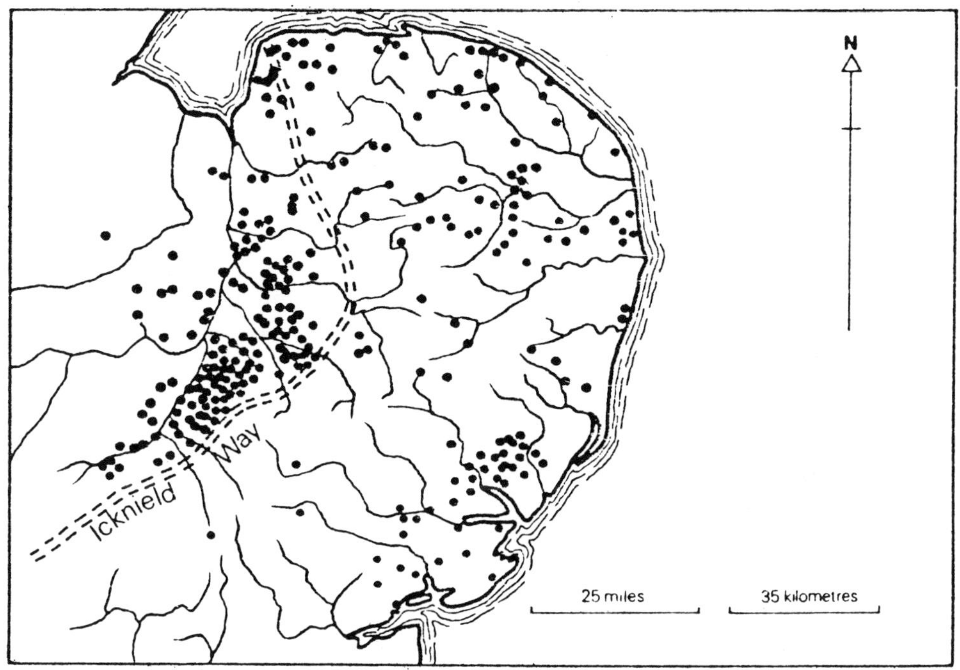

Fig. 6. Distribution of Neolithic stone tools found in East Anglia and originating in other parts of Britain. The line of the Icknield Way is marked, and the general spread of Neolithic artifacts is shown not to be restricted to the Way itself.

The whole operation of natural routes in Britain was concerned, I think, with utilising firm, dry ground even if it was quite heavily wooded. Even rather feeble and incomplete maps of Bronze Age settlements in the south of England show a quite striking attention to the upland edges, and a comparable situation can today be seen in Denmark, where the uplands, such as they are, bear the scattered traces of old traffic. However—and this is more important for us—where the Danish ridges were truncated by streams and valleys, the tracks can be seen to converge down, the ruts deepen, and single places were often used, over long periods of time, to get across the base of the valley, or the muddy, marshy areas. The growth of peat has in some cases preserved not only the ruts, but in places also the attempts to lay a road, by wood, or more often stone paving. Dating is notoriously difficult, but clearly some at least are of prehistoric age. A paved surface laid on heavier rocks at Ellemose in Zealand is dated by lost artifacts to the Early Iron Age; it extends for only

150 m across the narrowest part of a fen. Another well made road, at Broskov, also in Zealand, is dated by artifacts to *c.* A.D. 400 and it too crosses a narrow fen, then fans out to meet a number of rutted tracks coming down the slope towards the fen. I do not know of any serious work done in Britain on the potential information which could be gained by pursuing the natural ridgeways in England and in Scotland, and by examining the waterlogged or muddy crossing places, probably covered and protected by hill wash and other colluvium. The opportunities for research seem great, although the effort would have to be considerable.

It may have seemed strange that I have avoided mention of a well-known phenomenon, *The Old Straight Track,* a self-explanatory title of a book of such long tradition that it seems a natural part of any consideration of ancient roads. Unfortunately, to my mind, it is not natural in any way; by joining various bits of the landscape, such as monuments, steeples, and crossroads, lines can be drawn on any map, preferably of small scale, and can be extended to any length until they hit yet more human artifacts of various antique ages. When they do, yet another *O.S.T.* is 'discovered'. The virtues of this scheme are that it does not have to concern itself with chronology—always a bother—and it has the advantage of 360 degrees of the compass from any starting point; so, unencumbered by facts, the Old Straight Tracks go on and on. Perhaps the kindest comment to be made about this archaeological fringe study is that if we try hard to find something that never existed, then we are likely to find it if we are not too particular about its source or relevance. But this is a different circumstance from one where the archaeologist seeks to find something that he can legitimately argue or infer did exist, and ancient traffic and communication are two aspects of known antiquity and of certain importance to prehistoric societies.

Roads and Tracks

Although prehistorians may search for organised traffic and maintained passages, there is still very little firm evidence for entirely artificial lines of communication in prehistoric Britain; only in a few places where natural conditions dictated that some deliberate effort was made to create a route has the evidence survived. And to these deliberate efforts I now turn. I think that in seeking to examine prehistoric roads and tracks, we should pay rather less attention to short entrances to settlements, internal paths and roadways, and more to lines of communication across long stretches of the land. There are of course many sites in this country and elsewhere, where hamlets, farmsteads and forts had internal footpaths or even provision for wagon or cart entry; a spectacular example is Biskupin in Poland, with a well-built internal road and paths, and the Iron Age settlement at Borremose in Jutland had, and still has, a metalled path leading into and through it, just as the settlement at Maiden Castle in Dorset had a form of road surfacing, of pounded pebbles.

Of earlier date are the Bronze Age trackways which linked farmsteads to fields in many parts of Britain (fig. 7). On the chalklands of southern England, many such internal systems existed, and sometimes they are complex; at Shearplace Hill in Dorset, for example, several sunken tracks spread out from the farmstead,

Fig. 7. Sketch plan of later Bronze Age fields and trackways at Dole's Hill, Dorset, to show the relationship of fields and tracks, and the organisation of the land.

providing clear and orderly approaches to some of the small fields worked from the farm. And similar hollow-ways or sunken tracks may extend for over 1000 m in countryside in both north and south Britain where recent agricultural or other activities have allowed them to survive, and where archaeologists have been aware of their existence. Again, much remains to be done and we have yet to discover such tracks in sufficient lengths and clear directions that we can begin to talk of planned and maintained communication systems. The time may not be too far away when this evidence will begin to emerge; the widespread clearance of forests in the Bronze Age probably opened up many new potential routes across the land, as well as diverting traffic from some old-established routes now shown to be longer or less convenient than new routes. We certainly need far more evidence of these Bronze Age tracks both in the soft chalklands of the south and on the hardrocks of upland areas to west and north.

Finally let us turn to proper undoubted made roads, which survive in many parts of the British Isles, particularly in Ireland, certainly in England, perhaps in Scotland and Wales, and which demonstrate both purposeful manufacture and direction, and which therefore give us some idea about land transport and communication in prehistoric times. We need these made roads to allow us that precision about the movement and passage of humans, animals and goods that we can get from no other sources (fig. 8). All of these made roads are of wood, sometimes with a stone base or support, but essentially of wooden poles fitted together to make either a rigid, or a flexible, structure. Thousands and thousands of these may have existed in Britain and Ireland, across moor, marsh and mud, but only those which were subsequently buried by wet deposits, especially peat, have survived. All the rest have rotted away.

In eastern England, many such made roads existed once, but most are now destroyed by peat shrinkage and drying out. One of them once joined Bronze Age settlements on the Isle of Ely with those on the major uplands to the south; all that survived were the oak piles, dragged up in past years by the farmer. The same general class of structures has been noted in Ireland, Yorkshire, north-west England and in Scotland too, in Flanders Moss and in the south-west of Scotland, but as usual the dating of most of these is very imprecise, and certainly many of such wooden structures were of recent date.

Fig. 8. Reconstruction of trackway and landscape in the Somerset Levels, based upon excavations and environmental studies.

One area of Britain where many such tracks are known to have existed is Somerset, where in an area of about 400 square miles we have information about many prehistoric made roads. The existence of these tracks shows the organisation of prehistoric societies in making and maintaining communication networks, and they also demonstrate the complexity and ingenuity that went into the tracks themselves. Because these tracks in Somerset are so well preserved, they demonstrate the range, the quality and perhaps the quantity of such ancient tracks in Britain as a whole. They should serve to alert some of those working on the land, including field archaeologists, to the possibilities for new discoveries.

The earliest known track in Somerset, and the earliest made road in the world, is the Sweet Track, a structure running for hundreds of metres between two settlement areas of the fourth millennium bc, in other words, not a short entry to a settlement but a proper system which linked two areas. The fitting together of the various components of this made road involved a rather ingenious set of wooden parts, rails, pegs, planks, more pegs and posts to make a raised walkway, an elevated track, above the watery and flooded swamp (fig. 9). The trees for the planks were oak and ash, felled by fire and stone axe, split and wedged, perforated and notched by axe; some of these trees were *c.* 300 years old, i.e. they were substantial trees of up to four metres circumference. The structure was put together by combining freshly felled wood, for both timber and round wood, and quite importantly we know that at least two different stands of timber were being felled, and at least two different gangs of workmen made the Track; we also know that Neolithic 'surveyors' went first and laid out the line of the track, marking it with posts and providing a duckboard walkway in order to allow the loads of timber to be brought on site. The workers were fed on site, at least we presume so, and we have several Neolithic pots, one filled with hazelnuts, dropped accidentally along the way while the track was being built. We do not have the ceremonial cutting of the ribbon to open the motorway (although we did find one piece of Neolithic rope, at the very end of the track!). The whole enterprise, in fact, gives an impression of a quite orderly set of instructions and a well-managed and well-supplied piece of work. The Sweet Track lasted maybe 20–30 years, and then it was abandoned to the marsh and the growth of the peat which eventually extended to about six metres thickness over the track, hence its preservation until today.

This track is only one of a multitude of such structures in the Somerset Levels, and in Britain. As it happens to be the most complex in structural variety as well as the earliest, it deals a hard blow to those who see the evolution of human industry in terms of simple to elaborate, basic to complex. The fact is, of course, that prehistoric people were far too clever for such predictable practices, and they did what had to be done in whatever manner they wanted to.

By the third and second millennium bc, a quite astonishing series of networks of roads and tracks must have existed in Britain; we know something of the network segments in Somerset, in East Anglia, in north-west England and parts of Ireland, but many areas including Scotland remain to be explored for these traces. Only if we can discover or deduce further segments can we begin to talk of any organisation of traffic wider than a purely local or regional one. Nonetheless, small networks must have linked settlements on the dry chalklands of southern England, and on the limestone, sands and rocks of other regions, although the exact routes and the precise

Fig. 9. Early Neolithic track in the Somerset Levels—the Sweet Track. Dated to the late fourth millennium bc, this Track linked settlements on the Polden Hills and an island in the middle of the swamp. The line was first marked out by long posts driven into the peat, and thereafter the heavy timbers were brought down from the hills and placed in position.

Fig. 10. Late Neolithic road in the Somerset Levels—the Abbot's Way. Dated to 2000 bc, this simple structure linked settlements on two islands in the raised bog of the Levels. Over 30,000 planks were used, most of them roughly split from alder.

character of these roads are not yet known. In our wetlands, such tracks have survived and we can therefore get a close idea of what was involved, where the roads were, how they were built, what they linked. The variation in these wooden constructions is great, from brushwood tracks and junctions to multiple single lines, including well over one hundred track lines in one area of Somerset, or single lines of more heavily built and substantial roadways, snaking their way across the landscape. One of these, the Abbot's Way, dated to 2000 bc, runs for about 2,500 m and was made of about 30,000 planks each about one metre long; the road was made as a single unit in one period of activity on the part of the community (fig. 10). Another road, this time of the Bronze Age and *c.* 1000 bc, was 2,500 m long and linked the Polden Hills with the central island of

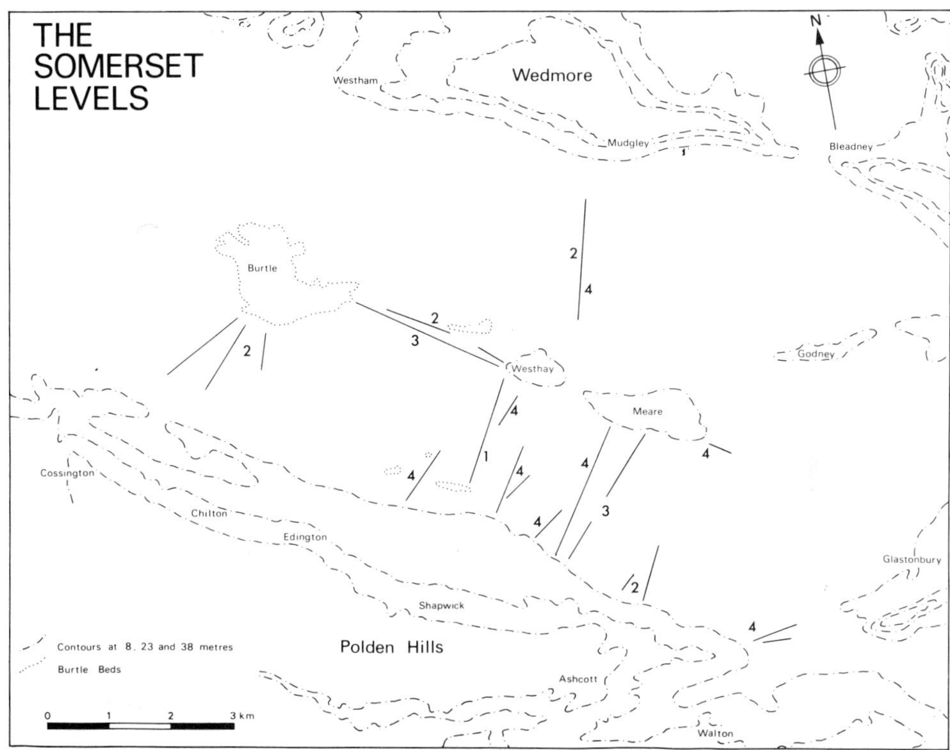

Fig. 11. Distribution of major prehistoric roads and tracks in the northern part of the Somerset Levels. The structures are varied in both the woods used and the methods of fitting them together. They are roughly grouped on this map by radiocarbon age: 1, Early Neolithic, 3200 bc. 2, Later Neolithic, 2800–2200 bc. 3, Late Neolithic and Early Bronze Age, 2000–1500 bc. 4, Later Bronze Age, 1200–500 bc. Roads of the present day follow many of the prehistoric routes very closely.

Meare; it needed many thousands of oak planks, but all, we think, came from only 60–65 mature oak trees, such was the apparent care in the woodworking. Perhaps some plan for conservation of resources, already scarce according to the tree ring stresses, may be apparent here.

But the networks are important, and here in Somerset, as doubtless elsewhere, we can see a Neolithic (third millennium) plan, and a Bronze Age (*c.* 1000 bc) plan (fig. 11) and we can compare these with the modern road map and not be surprised that we today follow the selfsame lines, choosing the shortest and most convenient routes, repairing and maintaining the roads, and keeping open the links between settlements, supplies and land. The comparison between ancient routes and modern routes is not a subject to pursue here, but there is no doubt in my mind that, for example, the historic road systems of Scotland must throw some light, and many suggestions, on the likely routes chosen by prehistoric inhabitants of Scotland.

Conclusion

At the beginning I repeated statements made by many experts, that apart from a brief episode during the Roman occupation, Britain and western Europe had no road networks of a fixed and permanent character until very late, perhaps 300–400 years ago. Those areas where the evidence is well-preserved begin to suggest that organised local communication systems did exist well before the Roman Conquest, and they therefore provide suggestions about the nature of the societies that made them.

But for prehistoric Britain, the evidence of established roads and tracks is sparse, and we are forced to rely upon other evidence of a less precise kind, the presumed existence of great natural routes, and the possible networks now seen only as incomplete archaeological maps of artifacts. Prehistorians accept that what they can actually see is quite likely to be only the tip of what there was, preserved (as are the wooden roads) by accident, by freak of nature, by great good fortune. In waterlogged regions such as Somerset, we can see many prehistoric wooden tracks and roads, but elsewhere there were without doubt many well-established, maintained, dry land routes, linking settlements, industrial workshops, markets, farmsteads; just because we cannot actually see them is no reason to say they did not exist, and far worse is to ignore them in our studies of the working of ancient societies. The whole history and prehistory of human society depended upon contact and communication, transmission of goods, ideas and genes; to ignore the precision offered by a study of routes and roads would seem to represent a failure on the part of the archaeologist who seeks to understand the nature of past societies.

Further Reading

Details of the prehistoric wooden roads and trackways in the Somerset Levels may be found in *Somerset Levels Papers*, **1–10** (1975–1984), and a more general description is now avavailable in Coles, J.M. and Orme, B.J., *Prehistory of the Somerset Levels* (1980).

A summary of some of the evidence for ancient routes has recently appeared, unfortunately without references: Taylor, C.C., *Roads and Tracks of Britain* (1979).

The evidence for traffic by sea, including references to some of the Scottish archaeological distributions, appears in Johnstone, P., *The Sea-craft of Prehistory* (1980).

Sources of Illustrations

Fig. 1. Wright, J.V., *Ontario Prehistory* (National Museums of Canada, 1972).

Fig. 2. Ashbee, P., *The Ancient British* (Geo Abstracts Ltd, 1978).

Fig. 3. Megaw, J.V.S. and Simpson, D.D.A., *Introduction to British Prehistory* (Leicester University Press, 1979).

Fig. 4. Collis, J.R., in Jesson, M. and Hill, D. (eds.), *The Iron Age and its Hill-Forts* (University of Southampton, 1971).

Fig. 5. *Proceedings of the Prehistory Society,* **37** (1971).

Figs. 6–7. Taylor, C.C., *Roads and Tracks of Britain* (J.M. Dent & Sons Ltd., 1979).

Fig. 8. Coles, J.M. and Orme, B.J., *Prehistory of the Somerset Levels* (1980).

Figs. 9–11. Author.

The Evidence from the Roman Period

G.S. Maxwell

To handle so extensive a subject as the above in the compass of a few brief pages without savagely compressing the wealth of detailed information that exists is a well-nigh impossible task. Of equal difficulty is the presentation of that précis without giving the erroneous impression that the present state of our knowledge makes an approach to completeness. In this, as in so many other topics relating to Romano-British archaeology, we are barely at the surface of things; the deeper, more satisfying truths wait to be uncovered at some future date.

But we can be clear about some things. For example, it is important to appreciate that in considering Roman roads side by side with prehistoric tracks or medieval thoroughfares, we are not strictly comparing like with like. Roman roads were the deliberate product of the military mind: a uniform system, constructed by standardised methods and with carefully selected materials; designed to serve, almost literally, as the sinews of war.

Even a cursory glance at a schematic diagram of the Roman road-network in Scotland (fig. 12) suffices to show that it was intended to provide an arterial system by which the vital life-blood of an army of occupation, that is men and supplies, could be transported quickly from one area of the lowland zone to another. Such a role implies that the roads were an integral part of the machinery of occupation, and that to study them adequately we should also consider the structures which they linked together, and, indeed, the troops and vehicles that travelled over them. This is impossible here, but we can touch briefly upon a few salient points, dealing particularly with the surviving physical remains. But first, a short sketch of the historical background.

The Roman army first entered Scotland around A.D. 80, in the governorship of Julius Agricola. By 84 most of lowland Scotland, up to and including Strathmore, had been made part of the province. In A.D. 86 or 87, however, events compelled the emperor Domitian to abandon the northernmost area of Agricolan conquest, and only southern Scotland remained within the Imperial frontiers. A few

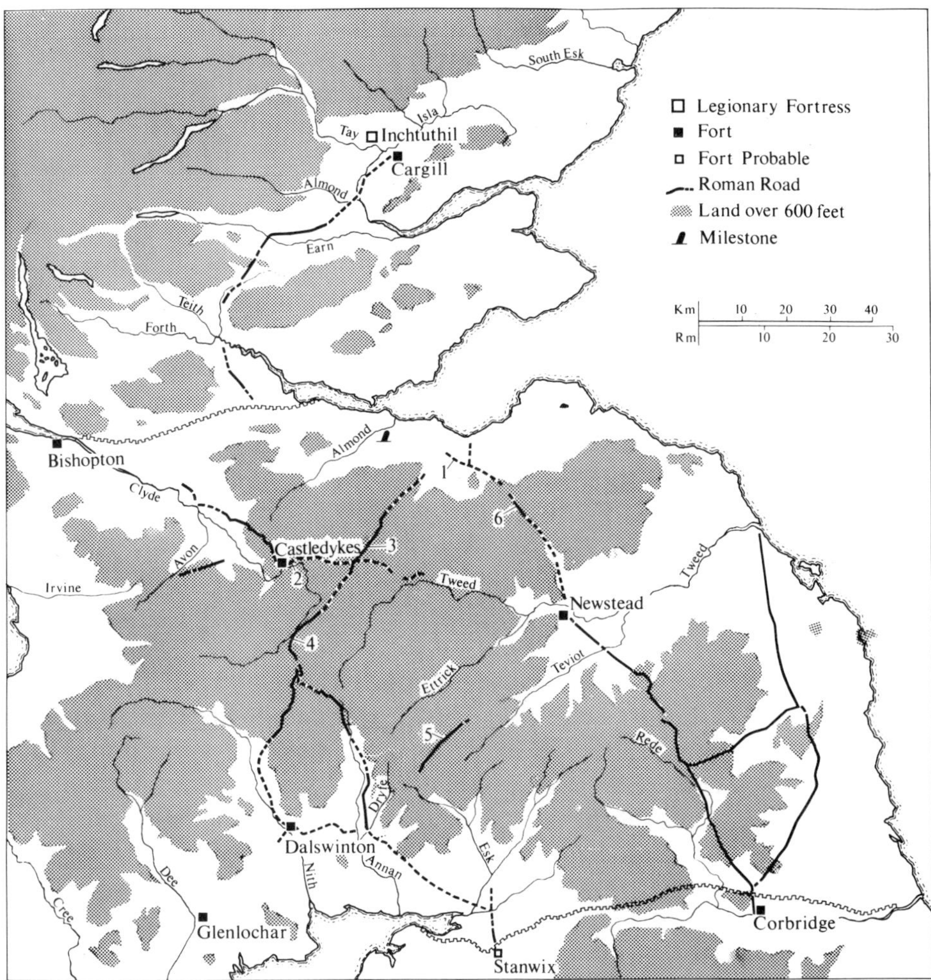

Fig. 12. The Roman road-system in Scotland, with selected forts. Sectors described in greater detail numbered: 1. Dere Street, Elginhaugh; 2. near Castledykes; 3. at Ingraston; 4. at Wandel; 5. on Craik Moor; 6. Dere Street, near Soutra.

years after the start of the second century the 'Domitianic' phase came to an end, and the boundary of Roman power was withdrawn to the Tyne-Solway line, where it remained until, under Antoninus Pius in the early 140s, Scotland was re-occupied as far north as the Tay. On this occasion a running barrier, the Antonine Wall, was built from Forth to Clyde, and there the position rested, with only a brief interval, until the 160s. Then, as previously, the Scottish installations began to be abandoned, so that some time before the end of the second century the frontier once more straddled the southern isthmus. Finally, for a few years after A.D. 208, as a result of the Caledonian campaigns of the emperor Septimius Severus and his son Caracalla, a number of forts on the eastern side of the country were held as outposts. The rest is darkness.

In none of these periods can the nature and purpose of the road-system be properly understood without an appreciation of the wide range of installations that are to be found intimately connected with it.[1] For example, disposed at regular intervals along the roads, there were *castella*, garrison-posts capable of accommodating 500–1,000 men, but occasionally, and especially in the Southern Uplands, occupied by subdivisions or vexillations of whole regiments, probably not more than 250 men in strength. At intermediate positions between these there could also be smaller road posts: fortlets, holding between 50 and 100 troops, and, as occasion demanded, linking these in turn, a range of timber watch-towers and signal-stations, each manned by not more than a handful of troops.

Adjacent to several of the larger forts, as at Newstead,[2] there were also *mansiones*, the well-equipped resting-places of imperial couriers and government agents, posting on the *cursus publicus* for the purpose of assessment and inspection of provincial affairs. And there were, too, those utilitarian reminders of the Imperial authority upon which all depended, the milestones, recording the name of the Emperor in whose reign they were set up. To each of these installations the road was a necessary adjunct, for most a basic condition of existence.

Along these roads poured a constant stream of traffic, persons and vehicles, employed in the defence, administration or provisioning of the northernmost military zone of Britannia. Symbolic of this ceaseless flow is the well-worn north gateway of Housesteads fort on Hadrian's Wall, the threshold stone eroded by the passage of innumerable carts and wagons, their wheeltrack approximating so closely to the British railways' standard gauge of 4 ft 8½ in. Recent excavations at Ardoch have revealed a section of road rutted by vehicles of a similar track, and amongst the finds from many *castella* in Scotland are the corroded fragments of iron furnishings from the early wagons that may have produced similar ruts: iron tyres, linch-pins, hub-mountings (fig. 13)—even, as at Newstead and Balmuildy,

Fig. 13. Iron furnishings of wheeled vehicles from the Roman fort at Newstead.

the remains of wooden wheels showing a high degree of craftsmanship in their fabrication. The illustrated example, from Newstead (fig. 14), has a felloe made from a single piece of ash. The manufacture of such wheels demanded skilful handling of materials, and in Diocletian's day they fetched a price ten times higher than that of a wheel made with a composite felloe.[3] Whether or not the vehicles to which these wheels belonged were of Roman or Celtic origin—and it must be remembered that even the Latin names for most forms of wheeled transport stemmed from Celtic sources—there can be no doubt that such vehicles formed a sufficiently high proportion of the traffic to make their presence a modifying constraint on the design and construction of the road-system. For, whereas the passage of human and animal road-users contributed only in a relatively small way to the gradual wear and tear of roads—possibly even helping to compact the upper metalling, the iron tyres of heavily-laden, unsprung vehicles, by digging into the smooth running-surfaces, effectively accelerated the erosive

Fig. 14. Wooden wheel from the Roman fort at Newstead.

processes of frost and surface-drainage. Moreover, the severity of wear would have been even more marked on gradients, for the amount of power put forth by a draught-animal pulling a load (and thereby the amount of stress imposed upon the road-surface) is directly proportional to the gradient up which the load is being moved. Thus, the force required to pull a wagon along a level metalled surface is equivalent to about one-thirtieth of the all-up-weight, but the force needed to lift the load up a gradient of only 1 in 30 is twice as much. For one of 1 in 10 it is more than four times as much. With these factors in mind, we can appreciate the importance of skilful engineering and robust construction in the preparation of the Roman road-system in Scotland, much of it embracing the Border hills.

There are, in fact, few regions which offer better opportunities for studying the technical expertise and painstaking thoroughness of the Roman road engineer, partly because the problems imposed by the terrain have challenged him to exercise the full range of his considerable powers, partly because the pattern of subsequent land-use has been more favourable (until recent years) to the survival of their remains. Originally there may have been about 450 lineal miles of roadway in Roman Scotland; now only a tiny fraction remains, but it lies, for the most part, amongst the most attractive countryside in Great Britain.

The basic framework, probably conceived and laid down during the Agricolan period, is very simple: from Corbridge the main road, now known as Dere Street, was driven northwards over Cheviot by way of Redesdale, across the valleys of Teviot and Tweed, and up Lauderdale to the shores of the Forth; from Carlisle a second main axis of communication led via Annandale and Upper Clydesdale along the south-east shoulder of the Pentland Hills to meet the first, probably within the confines of what is now the City of Edinburgh. Thence a single route drove westwards to Stirling, where it crossed the River Forth, turned north by way of Strathallan to cross the River Earn near Crieff, and then led north-eastwards to ford the Tay near its confluence with the Almond. How far it was intended to continue up the left bank of the Tay, and so into Strathmore, is not known. Certainly the road seems to have been constructed as far as Cargill at the junction of Tay and Isla, opposite the legionary fortress of Inchtuthil, but the evidence of its course beyond this point is far from incontrovertible. It is possible that when the Domitianic reversal of policy occurred in A.D. 86/7 the road-building programme had not reached either the garrisons on the outermost frontier or those hinterland forts lying away from the main trunk-routes. Doubtless, however, it was intended that the road should continue by way of Cardean and Finavon at least as far as Stracathro on the North Esk, if not some terminal station on the Bervie Water. The system just described catered for most of the north-south traffic in Scotland. The main east-west route utilised the natural advantages offered by the valleys of Tweed, Clyde, Avon and Irvine, thus connecting the important garrisons at Loudoun Hill, Castledykes, Lyne (or Easter Happrew), and Newstead. The logical extension of this road at either end, westwards to Irvine on the Firth of Clyde, and eastwards to the very mouth of the Tweed, would also have given direct access to fine harbourage facilities.

Subsidiary loops or spurs also probably planned or built in the first century included the following, which bound outlying garrisons into the main network: one route diverged from the Annandale trunk near Lockerbie and, driving westwards to the Nith a little way above Dumfries, led north up the left bank of the river to

Durisdeer, at which point it climbed north-east over the watershed into the valley of the Potrail and the Daer Water, thus rejoining the north-south trunk-route at Crawford in Clydesdale. It is possible that a spur diverged from this loop at Dalswinton to cross the River Nith and continue southwestwards towards Glenlochar on the Dee. Another transverse route, probably not built until the Antonine period, left the Annandale road at the foot of Dryfesdale and struck out north-east across the hills by way of Craik Moor to provide direct communication with Newstead, which at all periods may be considered the hub of the road-system in Scotland. This route in turn was joined by a spur, which cut through upper Eskdale to link Newstead with the major bases at Stanwix and Carlisle by way of Broomholm and Netherby. Another addition likely to have been made in the second century was the road which left the main east-west artery north-west of Castledykes to proceed down Clydesdale to the central isthmus, where, probably at Balmuildy, it must have joined the Military Way; this was primarily intended to serve the garrisons on the Antonine Wall, but it fulfilled a double purpose in that it provided yet another east-west link, giving access to harbours on either coast. Finally, there is evidence of a route, or at least a patrol-track, extending west along the left bank of the Clyde from near Bishopton, to provide a means of communication for the garrisons guarding the exposed left flank of the Antonine Wall.

Other routes doubtless wait to be discovered or confirmed, but these represent the main elements; it is now time to consider the nature of the surviving remains. What do they look like? How does one recognise them?

Proverbially, one of the main distinguishing characteristics of a Roman road is its straightness:

> Straight as a rule before him lay
> For many a mile the Roman way.

As a description, this may have sufficed for Walter Scott or William of Deloraine, but there are in fact relatively few surviving stretches in Scotland to which this criterion may be applied. The sector of Dere Street between Ulston Moor and Lilliard's Edge in Roxburghshire is an outstanding example. Most of the better-preserved stretches, however, are situated in rolling uplands where the terrain prevents it. Nevertheless, even here the rectilinearity—the principle of point-to-point alignment in the laying out of the road—still holds good, although it must be noted that the straight stretches are often quite short.

The means used for establishing the alignment would have varied, according to the accuracy required or the distance involved. For most purposes visual sighting from one prominent landmark to another, the Eildon Hills for example, or Kippit Hill on the Pentlands road, would have sufficed, the specific line being determined by ranging with rods, flags or, it has even been suggested, movable beacons. If necessary, however, the surveyor could resort to astronomical calculations, involving observation of sun or stars, and a wide range of sighting and levelling instruments was available to help him: the *groma*, for example, a rudimentary but efficient sighting cross-staff, or the *dioptra*, which could be used for measuring angles and heights—the latter being particularly useful for engineering a road through hill country, where gradients were critical. Few examples of these survive, but it has been suggested that the enigmatic *dodecahedra*,[4] twelve-sided bronze objects with a hole of different size in each face, could have been used for work of this nature. And, of course, it must be remembered that the surveyors would have been military personnel, highly-trained specialists whose like was not to be seen again in Scotland for more than a thousand years.

Another distinguishing characteristic commonly referred to is the presence of a broad *agger*, a bank of material cast up from quarry ditches on either side to form a raised bed on which the running surface itself could be laid. Such structures, as used for Roman arterial routes in the lowland zone of Britain, frequently bulk large in the present-day landscape, even when attenuated by cultivation or decay; examples on Ermine Street, Stane Street and elsewhere attain a width of 15 to 20 m and rise to a maximum height of 2 m above the surrounding ground. This scale of construction, however, is rarely seen in Scotland—although instances of comparable methods are known in places on Dere Street—one of the reasons for its absence being that the *agger* is really meant for use in level ground to provide a firm, well-drained base upon which to lay the lowest levels of the street itself, and in most of the surviving sectors in Scotland, and indeed generally in north Britain, it was more practicable to construct the entire road-bed of heavy boulder bottoming—a material which mostly lay ready to hand—and to base it directly on the subsoil.

Whatever the nature of its base or bottoming, the upper surface of the metalling, usually cobbles and grit or rammed gravel, normally exhibits a camber, and the crown of the causeway is frequently observed to be stiffened by a pronounced mid-rib, the whole being held together by kerbing of considerable weight. Surface-water cast off by the camber was collected in ditches, often of no great size, and, on sloping ground, culverts were provided to convey excess storm-water beneath the road and away from the uphill side, thus diminishing the dangers of a wash-out. Drainage-ditches are clearly to be distinguished from the broad quarry-ditches already mentioned, as are marking-out ditches, set back some distance from the metalled road; the function of the latter appears to have been to define what Margary called a 'road-zone',[5] which would doubtless have been kept free from vegetation and may even have been reserved for 'parking', although only at Ardoch has anything corresponding to the 'hard shoulder' of modern highways been detected, and this on a relatively small scale.[6] In general, the side-ditches were slight affairs, and in most cases they are no longer, or only faintly, visible.

More likely to survive are the quarries from which the material for the running-surface was derived. These generally appear as small circular or oval pits, now relatively shallow, set back some way from the road—in sloping ground usually on the uphill side; in one set of examples on the road north of Moffat, the pits possess short ramps, up which the quarried stone or gravel was carried to the nearby road. Where quarrying activity has been particularly intense, the pits frequently appear to coalesce, merging into one another to form a series like a string of beads; they present a distinct and useful contrast to the larger, more widely separated quarries that accompany many eighteenth-century and later roads. However, it must be remembered that there was a considerable degree of variation in the methods employed to apply the above principles of construction—as many variations, in fact, as there are types of terrain over which the road had to be engineered.

The recently discovered stretch of road at Elginhaugh, Midlothian (NT 320673, fig. 15a), near the crossing of the North Esk, revealed on excavation a remarkably well-preserved example of a basal *agger*. Measuring approximately 12 m in width, the *agger* was composed almost entirely of a sandy brown loam which contained very few stones of any size. The subsoil at this point was a mixed

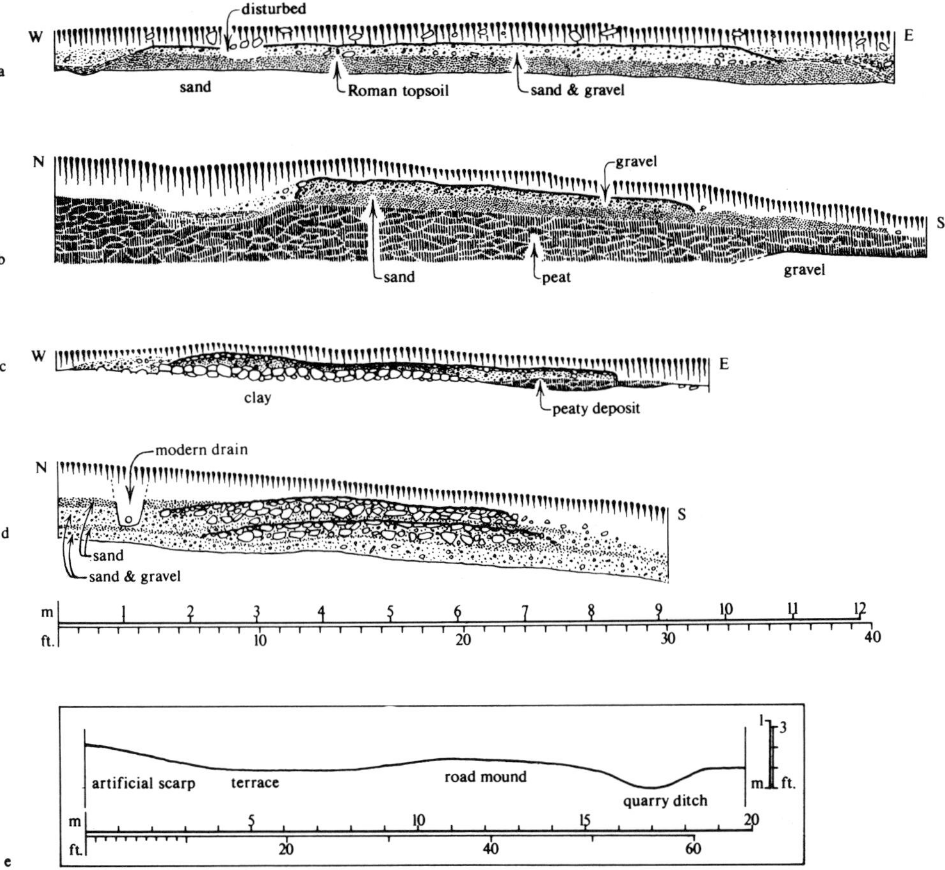

Fig. 15 (a–e). Sections of Roman roads: a. Dere Street, Elginhaugh; b. at Ingraston; c. at Wandel; d. at Castledykes; e. Dere Street, near Soutra.

sandy gravel, interspersed with pockets of fine running sand. There were obviously no drainage problems in such a porous material, and consequently the side ditches were little more than gutters, but the yielding nature of the stone-free areas crossed by the road probably made necessary the construction of a relatively substantial *agger*. Similar considerations presumably led to a more elaborate substructure in the second example (fig. 15d), where hill-wash has almost totally obscured the profile of a remarkably well-preserved section of the main east-west trunk-route a little to the east of Castledykes in Clydesdale (NS 938444).[7] Here the road, in obliquely descending the face of an escarpment, appears, now as a slight terrace, betrayed by a bump in hedge or fence-line, now as a broad swelling that bridges the frequent transverse gullies in its path. Before constructing the road in such gullies, a 'raft' or local *agger* of earth, sand and gravel has been laid to infill the deepest parts of the depression. Upon this a bedding layer of sand, then boulder road-bottoming and, in turn, upper cobble and grit have been laid. Evidently, though, the superincumbent weight led to subsidence, and in due course a second *agger*, another sand-bed and an upper street were constructed on top of the first. It would be satisfying to think that the two surfaces represented roads of the Flavian and Antonine periods respectively, but there is nothing to give a firm date in either case.

Difficulties of a different kind were encountered at Ingraston, Tweeddale (NT 116484),[8] immediately north-west of the village of Dolphinton. A section of the Roman road exposed in trenches cut for a new field drainage system (fig. 15b) showed that it had been constructed on top of a layer of peat, itself overlying running sand. In such a situation heavy bottoming was clearly out of the question, and even the uppermost layers could not have included more than a small proportion of stone, for fear that the whole structure might subside. In the event, relatively thin layers of sand or gravel seem to have sufficed; although the uppermost surface was badly worn, the absence of cobbles and large stones in the adjacent parts of the field—also traversed by drainage cuts—indicated that the road was never substantially metalled. The constructional technique appears to have been successful enough at this point, at the top of a gentle incline, but a little way to the south-west, where the line of the road led round the foot of Kippit Hill, an abundance of surface-water, formerly known to locals as the Devil's Sweat, evidently caused it to sink, and when uncovered by roadworks in 1972 the original metalled surface was covered by a peaty deposit about 0.3 m deep.

In sectors where the lines of the road now run through long-established arable, or where centuries of travellers have been compelled by the nature of the terrain to follow the Roman route quite closely, severe denudation and even complete destruction often occur for a considerable distance. Identifying the intermittent fragments may then pose a problem, and often the nature of the remains can only be assessed by their relationship to other structures. Such a case was observed at Wandel in Lanarkshire (NS 944268), where surface traces of the road identified by St

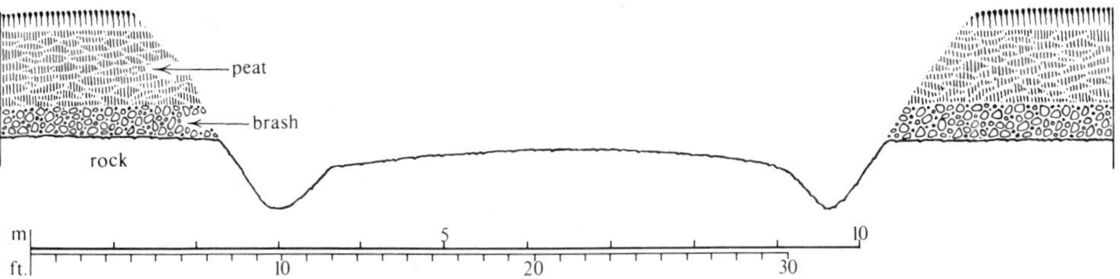

Fig. 16. Roman road cutting on Craik Moor (after Richmond).

Joseph in 1938 had been attenuated by recent ploughing, and only the prolongation of a section cut through the defences of an adjacent Roman fortlet revealed precise location of the causeway. Excavation (fig. 15c) showed that only 4.2 m of the original road-width could be recognised, virtually all the western half having been ploughed away. It is probable that the surviving portion owed its existence to the fact that, being built directly on a pure clay subsoil, and situated within the deeper part of a natural hollow, it may have lain in boggy ground unattractive to the early farmer. The peaty deposit which formed at the east edge of the road in Roman times would seem to confirm this, although there is no such formation above the cobble and gravel layer that covers the peat; the former may represent an attempt to provide a 'hard shoulder' at some later, undated, period of the road's use. It would be pleasant, however, to think that such road improvements, so familiar a scene to modern wayfarers, were also a routine task undertaken by the hard-working and ingenious Roman engineer.

Even more ingenuity is demonstrated on the Craik Moor road (fig. 16), where the basic rock, a shale, was covered by a layer of brash and further masked in places by a two-metre deposit of peat.[9] In this situation, the method adopted was to drive a deep cutting through both peat and brash and carve a cambered road-surface out of the living rock, almost 6 m wide and complete with side-ditches. On sloping ground, where the peat was absent, a level terrace 8 m wide was cut into the shale and the quarried spoil used to make a cambered road sitting on the artificial shelf. A similar technique was used in crossing the Raggengill Pass north of Crawford.

Appropriately, however, the finest engineering achievements are exhibited on Dere Street (figs. 17–18), especially in the stretch leading north from Newstead in the neighbourhood of Soutra. Here are displayed on a large scale the skills used to solve the problems

Fig. 17. Dere Street, Roman road at Windy Cleuch, Berwickshire.

also encountered on the Craik Moor. On sloping ground the road is carried on an artificial terrace as much as 17 m wide, and in one sector a cross-section of the 'road-zone' (fig. 15e) comprises a carefully-angled scarp, 4 m deep, on the uphill side; then a level 'berm' 4.5 m in breadth, the road-mound some 6 m wide, and finally, on the downhill side, a slack-bottomed ditch 3.5 m wide and almost a metre in depth.[10] Elsewhere in the vicinity there is evidence of Dere Street being based on a broad *agger* of clay,[11] and at Ulston Moor, several miles to the south of Newstead, a road-width of over 9 m is recorded. This is about half as wide again as the width of other roads in Roman Scotland and almost twice the width of the Military Way on the Antonine Wall, and it combines with the evidence of careful engineering visible at other points on the route to emphasise that Dere Street, together with its extension north of the Isthmus, was seen as the backbone of the entire system. The importance of Newstead as the main nodal point on that route is thereby also underlined.

Fig. 18. Dere Street, Roman road south of Teviot, crossing Roxburghshire.

It must not be thought that there is nothing new to be discovered about the Roman road-system in Scotland. On the contrary, there are many areas where much research still requires to be done—not least as regards the basic problem of the original extent of the network, especially in west and south-west Scotland, or in Strathmore, or even round Edinburgh itself, as the recent discoveries at Elginhaugh emphasise. We may expect that the patient application of persistent fieldwork will uncover missing fragments as the years go by. However, I have been impressed in recent years by just how much evidence may be collected in the course of aerial survey. And this extends not only to the identification of new sectors of road, but also to the discrimination between what is probably Roman and what is clearly of later date. Nothing is more difficult than to recognise an indubitably Roman origin in an isolated stretch of poorly preserved road—nothing, unless it be the attempt to disprove the veracity of a line hallowed by tradition.

At Huntingtower, near Perth, for example, parallel linear features were interpreted at an early stage of investigation either as a series of *cursus* monuments or as the side ditches of a Roman road-system of surprising complexity for such a northerly position, while an adjacent double row of pits was taken to be a prehistoric pit-alignment. More recent air photographs demonstrated, however, that the linear cropmarks, while probably associated with a road, were more likely to relate to an eighteenth- or nineteenth-century network than a Roman, while the pits differed markedly in character from the alignments of earlier native origin, being bigger, more shapeless, and less regularly disposed (fig. 19). Comparison with a stretch of authentic Roman road near Westerton, south of Crieff, is most instructive (fig. 20), for beside the westernmost row of quarry-pits, similarly shapeless and irregularly scattered, the penannular outline of a Roman watch-tower opening on to the road can clearly be seen. Curiously enough, there is no evidence at Westerton of yellowing caused by the presence of road-metalling, and, although it is possible that at this point it has been ploughed away completely, a photograph of the stretch of road immediately to the north, under pasture at the time of the sortie, showed by the distinct parching of the grass that the soil below contained a considerable proportion of stone debris. Similar parching betrayed the course of the road, including a sharp change of alignment, in the fields east of

Fig. 19. Roman roadside quarry-pits at Huntingtower revealed by cropmarks.

Crawford fort (fig. 21), and most recently at Elginhaugh, Dalkeith (fig. 22), where the presence of a T-junction and double change of alignment suggested that the road at that point might have entered the confines of a fort—an indication subsequently verified by excavation.[12] However, conditions of the opposite kind may also indicate the presence of a road. Overuse of the same course will in time lead to the destruction of the metalling and the formation of a hollow-way typical of the medieval and later type of thoroughfare. By their very nature hollow-ways act as reservoirs of moisture and

Fig. 20. Roman roadside quarry-pits at Westerton, south of Strageath, with watch-tower, revealed by cropmarks.

so produce darker markings in the ripening crop, as at Bar Hill on the Antonine Wall, for example, where the dark linear cropmark indicates the course of the Military Way, here, presumably, hollowed by post-Roman use into a sunken track (fig. 23).

Finally, at Inveresk on the Forth, two prints reveal the course of a ditched road following the right bank of the Esk and coming from the direction of Dalkeith, where Dere Street probably crossed the river; as it approaches the southern outskirts of the village, it

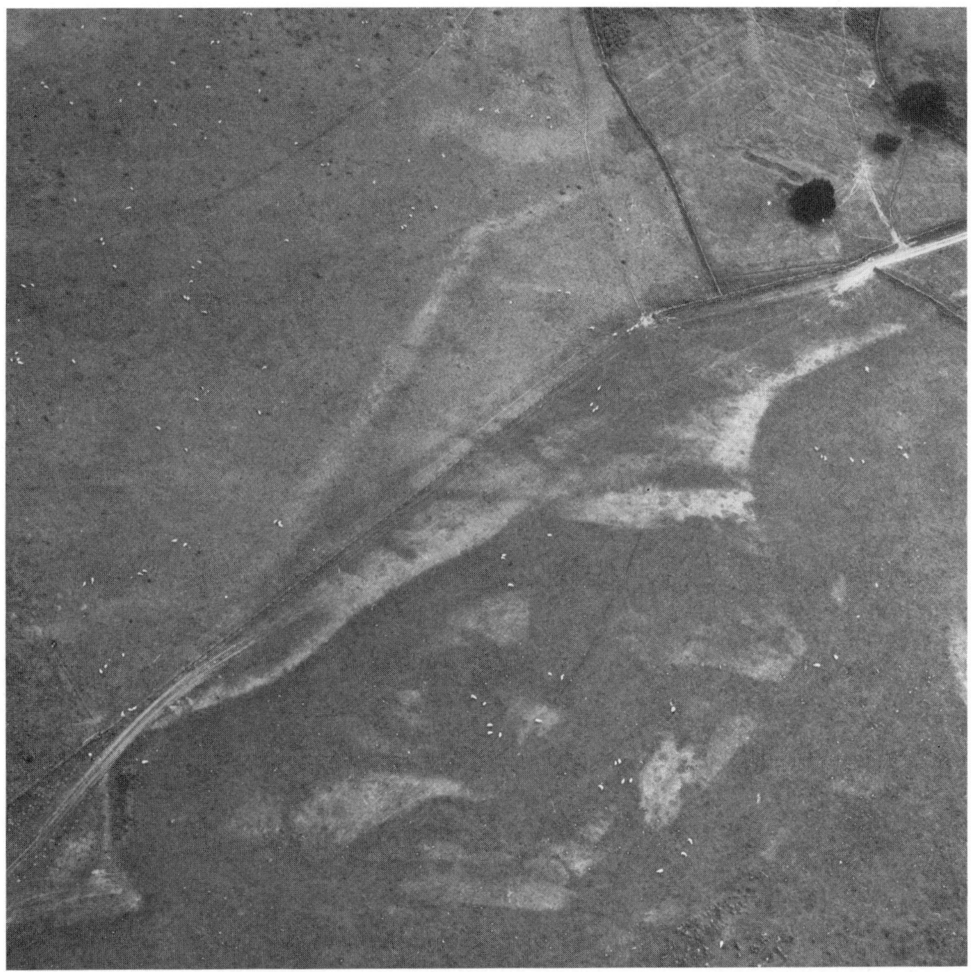

Fig. 21. Linear parchmark indicating course of Roman road immediately to the east of the fort at Crawford.

threads its way between the pens and enclosures of an ancient field-system (fig. 24). This is an area which has produced quite a quantity of Roman artifacts, amongst them a stone pine-cone finial from some as yet unrecognised funerary monument,[13] reminding us of yet another association with roads in Roman times, namely the burial of the dead. Tombstones and individual burials of Roman date have been discovered in the vicinity of a number of forts, but so far the precise location of a cemetery has eluded us. At Inveresk

Fig. 22. Linear parchmark indicating course of Roman road which issues from north-west gate of Elginhaugh fort; its alignment coincides with that of the modern highway A7, which appears to follow Dere Street from the Esk to Nether Liberton.

it is just possible that we may eventually identify a particularly interesting example.

Other road-associated features which it would be desirable to learn more about are the fords and bridges that must have existed throughout the country wherever the roads crossed water-courses of any size. Most of the latter were no doubt built entirely of timber, and nothing now remains apart from the abutments;[14] but it might

Fig. 23. Cropmark indicating course of the Military Way on the Antonine Wall to the east of Bar Hill.

be worthwhile excavating what appear to be the best-preserved examples to see if some structural evidence still survives. The best examples would be the crossings of the March Burn in Annandale (NT 042138), Air Cleuch on the Daer Water (NS 953154), or the Black Burn, Newtown St Boswells (NT 575320).

Stone was used in the abutments and piers of the Antonine bridge spanning the Kelvin at Balmuildy,[15] and the Tweed Bridge at

Fig. 24. Cropmarks of road at Inveresk traversing Romano-British field-system.

Newstead could have been of similar construction. However, it is not impossible that such an important crossing as the latter, at the present time graced by three delightful structures of widely differing ages, may have merited a bridge built entirely of stone. Old accounts[16] speak of handsome masonry pillaged from the 'arches' of a Roman bridge revealed when the water-level was low, but it is by no means safe to assume that the reference is to something more elaborate than piers or abutments of stone.

Another area which would repay further study is that of

gradients. Descriptive accounts of Roman routes may have much to say about constituent materials, or the exact course, alignments and so forth, but rarely do more than state that the road was carefully graded. Very few actually give facts and figures, which is a pity, because even superficial inspection of surviving stretches suggests that the Roman engineers themselves made an effort to produce a definite standard of grading. We have already seen that, in view of the type of traffic expected to use the road system, there were good reasons for trying to decrease the steepness of gradients. Where possible, this could be achieved by careful routing of the road, but in certain areas the ascent or descent of a naturally steep escarpment could not be avoided without an extensive detour. In this case, the road engineer had to consider both the overall effect of a long but relatively gradual slope and the practicability of a short, sharp variation in height. On Dere Street between Woden Law and Cappuck—the hilliest sector of the road—there are a good many precipitous scarps that have to be negotiated, but at none does traffic have to ascend a gradient steeper than 1 in 6 for more than 200 m; at the steepest points, the descent to Tow Ford and the ascent from the Mounthill Burn near Channelkirk, a slope of 1 in 4 has to be endured, but only for about 120 m. For longer slopes, such as that to the south of Whitton Edge or the descent from Turf Law to King's Inch at Soutra, gradients of 1 in 8 or 9 were apparently acceptable over distances of at least 400 m. On the Annandale route similar standards seem to have been observed: the steepest gradient on the climb north to Ericstane Hill is again 1 in 6; on the other hand the average natural slopes of 1 in 4 on either side of the Fopperbeck Burn, on the watershed between Clyde and Annan, have been negotiated by deft engineering on terraces of a gradient no steeper than 1 in 12. Again, at Crawford, where the road-builders avoided the narrow valley of the Clyde, the route climbs to the Raggengill Pass by a remarkable series of zig-zag terraces, so carefully graded as to be worthy of closer examination. The steepest natural slope is 1 in 3; the steepest road-gradient only 1 in 6, and half-way up the road runs level along the contour to give travellers a respite before the final haul to the summit. Comparison with Roman roads in Cumbria is instructive.[17] The fearful slopes on either side of the Hardknott Pass are traversed by a graded road that never exceeds 1 in 6 in steepness; immediately to the east, on the unavoidably vertiginous descent from the Three Shires Stone, the steepest gradient is 1 in 4, but only for 200 m. These were situations when we may be sure the best available surveyor's levels and hodometers would have been brought into use.

Finally, the question of date. At what stage of the occupation were these roads built? Only rarely is it possible to say with any certainty. Rudimentary track-preparation may have accompanied the earliest movement of troops in the area, as happened on the Jewish campaign in A.D. 68, according to Josephus. If the supply trains included wheeled vehicles of the sort depicted on Trajan's Column, some basic road-engineering may well have been demanded. However, the real road-construction programme must always have lagged some time behind the campaigning phase, for reasons of security if not shortage of available manpower; which is not to say that the time spent in early reconnaissance was not partly earmarked for the surveying of the road-system that was to come, as the practically unfailing association of roads and marching-camps would seem to suggest. Certainly it is true of the Flavian temporary camp at Silloans in Redesdale, where Dere Street has obviously been aligned to pass through the already-existing gateway of the Roman camp.[18] Another of the rare instances of material evidence relating to date is the quarry-pit of the Military Way at Bonnyside near Rough Castle.[19] This was infilled with turf-work and boulders by the builders of a beacon-stance which is integral with the curtain of the Antonine Wall, clearly indicating that rampart and road were being constructed at about the same time, probably around A.D. 142 and possibly just after the active campaigning had come to an end.

Most often, there is no direct testimony. Indeed, the only way one could obtain this is by the direct association of a milestone with the relevant stretch of road. But there is only one surviving example of a milestone in Scotland, the Ingliston stone,[20] and even this has no certain provenance. Commonly associated with Cramond, it was actually found near Ingliston House and may possibly indicate the approximate point at which the Roman road crossed the River Almond. What is most interesting about it is that it bears an inscription (fig. 25), dedicating it to the emperor Antoninus Pius and mentioning the unit of auxiliary troops who erected it as well as the Roman name for Newstead, *Trimontium*, showing that this was the *caput viae*, the hub of the road-system in southern Scotland. The text runs as follows:

[IMP(ERATORI) CAES(ARI) T(ITO)
AE(LIO) HADRI(ANO) ANTO]
NINO AVG(VSTO) PIO
P(ATRI) P(ATRIAE) CO(N)S(VLI) [I]II

[CO]H(ORS) I CVGERNOR(VM)
[TRI]MONTI(O) M(ILIA) P(ASSVVM)

Fig. 25. Roman milestone from Ingliston.

As to the date, it is only recently that the discovery of a missing fragment has allowed us to be certain that it was to Antonine that it referred. Even then there is some debate as to the exact Imperial consulship in which it was set up. Support has already been expressed for an early date, reading COS II rather than COS III in line 4, which would mean that the stone was erected by A.D. 139. It would be fascinating to think that Hadrian's Wall could have been abandoned, a victorious campaign fought, the country cleared of interloping barbarians and road-building begun all in the short space between the death of Hadrian in 138 and this early date. It would almost mean that Hadrian himself had made preparations just before his death for such a radical move; and that is a stimulating, if not a disturbing idea. But on second thoughts, it is probably best to believe with R.P. Wright that the correct date is 140 or later, and the road-construction falls into place beside work on the Antonine Wall and the Military Way. Yet, if so, we must still seek an explanation for the curious erasure in lines 5–6. It can only be the name of the provincial governor of the time, but why should his name suffer the dishonour of erasure, and who was he? It is generally reckoned that Lollius Urbicus was then governor in Britain, but his career, both then and subsequently, never merited such marks of disfavour. It must surely be his successor, and I am obliged to Professor Anthony Birley for bringing to my attention in this respect the existence of a Q Cornelius Priscianus, governor of Spain from A.D. 145, who was arraigned as a traitor for fomenting disorder in his province. It has been pointed out that Priscianus has a gap in his career between 142 and 145 which could appropriately be filled by the governorship of Britain. His could thus be the name and the title erased, and the road-building recorded would be assigned to that period. Here is yet another example of how deeply the archaeology of the Roman transport system in Scotland is embedded in the very heart of its history.

References

1. Cf. Collingwood, R.G. and Richmond, I.A., *The Archaeology of Roman Britain* (1969), 15–70.
2. Curle, J., *A Roman Frontier Post and its People* (1911), 92–103.
3. *J. Rom. Stud.*, **63** (1973), 105.
4. *Vereins Ingenieure Nachrichten*, 29 November 1961.

5. Margary, I.D., *Roman Roads in Britain* (3rd edn. 1973), 22.
6. *PSAS* (*Proceedings of the Society of Antiquaries of Scotland*), **102** (1969–70), 122–8.
7. *Glasgow Archaeol. J.*, **4** (1976), 93–8.
8. Noted by the author during the preparation of the Royal Commission's *Inventory of Lanarkshire* (1978).
9. *PSAS,* **80** (1945–6), 103–17.
10. RCAMS (Royal Commission on the Ancient Monuments of Scotland), *Inventory of Roxburghshire* (1956), **II,** 472.
11. *DES* (*Discovery and Excavation in Scotland*) (1964), 24.
12. *DES* (1980), 44; Maxwell, G.S., 'Recent aerial discoveries in Roman Scotland', *Britannia,* forthcoming.
13. *PSAS,* **13** (1878–9), 267–9.
14. *Archaeol. J.*, **118** (1961), 136–64.
15. Miller, S.N. (ed.), *The Roman Occupation of South-western Scotland* (1952), 88—94; the timbers dredged from the Kelvin at this point have now been dated by dendrochronology to A.D. 1360. However, there is no reason to doubt the origin of the traces of abutments or piers (*Glasgow Archaeol. J.*, **6** (1979), 65–6).
16. E.g. Milne, A., *A Description of the Parish of Melrose in Answer to Mr Maitland's Queries* (1769), 6.
17. *Trans Cumberland and Westmorland Antiq. and Archaeol. Soc.* (new series), **49** (1949), 15–26.
18. *A History of the County of Northumberland,* **15** (1940), 124–5.
19. *PSAS,* **90** (1956–7), 161–9.
20. Collingwood, R.G. and Wright, R.P., *The Roman Inscriptions of Britain* **1** (1965), No. 2313.

Further Reading

I. Roman Roads in Scotland

Crawford, O.G.S., *Topography of Roman Scotland* (1949), 1–9.

Macdonald, J., 'Notes on the "Roman" Roads of the one-inch Ordnance Map of Scotland: The Dumfriesshire roads', *PSAS* **38** (1893–4), 298–320.

Macdonald, J., 'Notes on the "Roman" Roads of the one-inch Ordnance Survey Map of Scotland: The Roxburghshire Roads', *PSAS* **29** (1894–5), 317–28.

Margary, I.D., *Roman Roads in Britain* (3rd edition, 1973), 452–523.

Miller, S.N. (ed.). *The Roman Occupation of South-western Scotland* (1952), 1–82.

RCAMS, *Inventory of Roxburghshire* (1956), **2,** 463–74.

RCAMS, *Inventory of Stirlingshire* (1963), **1,** 112–16.
RCAMS, *Inventory of Peeblesshire* (1967), **2,** 342–4.
RCAMS, *Inventory of Lanarkshire* (1978), 137–44.

II. Roman Roads in General

Chevallier, R., *Roman Roads* (1976).
Collingwood, R.G. and Richmond, I.A., *The Archaeology of Roman Britain* (1969), 1–7.
Crawford, O.G.S., *Archaeology in the Field* (1953), 60–86.
Ordnance Survey, *Ordnance Survey Professional Papers* (new series), **13,** 'Field Archaeology', 4th edition (1963), 90–3.
Sitwell, N.N.H., *Roman Roads of Europe* (1981).
Wacher, J., *Roman Britain* (1978), 187–90.

Land Routes: The Medieval Evidence

G.W.S. Barrow

A series of papers in the *Scottish Geographical Magazine* some twenty years ago on 'The Roads of Scotland'[1] proceeded directly from the period of Roman occupation to the Statute Labour Roads of the seventeenth century, with only the following perfunctory nod at the intervening eleven hundred years:

> After the Roman period no roads were made in Scotland until the seventeenth century, except the occasional 'causeway'. . . . Roads in the modern sense were not needed in medieval times, when all travelling was done on foot or on horseback, and merchandise was generally carried on packhorses. The few wheeled carts and waggons which were in use for the transport of heavy goods made very slow progress and in their place sleds (sledges) were often used.[2]

Now, it is undeniable that on the list of prerequisites for progress of which impatient eighteenth-century Scots felt their country to be in need an adequate system of carriage roads stood very high. On this question, for example, the words of the Reverend James Arkle, minister of Castleton in Roxburghshire, are striking only because of their graphic vigour, not because they are untypical:

> It must appear very strange to any person acquainted with the improvements, which other parts of Scotland have received by means of roads, when it is mentioned, that in this very extensive country not a yard of road had ever been attempted to be formed till within these few years. The statute labour has long been commuted. For about sixteen miles along the Liddal the road lay rather *in* the river than upon its banks, the only path being in what is called the Watergate and the unhappy traveller must cross it at least twenty-four times in that extent. . . . There is much intercourse with both Hawick and Langholm by weekly markets, fairs, etc. and the difficulty of travelling to those places is inconceivable. Every article must be carried on horseback; and through these deep and broken bogs and mosses we must crawl to the great fatigue of ourselves but the much greater injury of our horses without the hope of a more comfortable mode of travelling. As we have hitherto had no roads, it is not to be expected that we should have had bridges.[3]

Fig. 26. Bridge of Balgownie. Mid-19th century lithograph by Michel Bouquet. By permission of Aberdeen University Library.

But we are not entitled to assume that the parlous state of Scottish land communications in the eighteenth century had been an unchanging feature of the country over many centuries, still less since the last piece of highway maintenance had been completed by local labour squads under the direction of the last Roman road surveyor. We must look carefully at all the references to roads and highways in surviving record before we decide that all or any of them relate merely to footpaths, bridlepaths, packhorse trails or drove roads. While the converse of Mr Arkle's remark about the bridges is not valid—i.e., wherever there are bridges we cannot necessarily infer carriage roads, for bridges may have been built merely for packhorses or pedestrians—we ought nevertheless to look at all the evidence for bridges, as well as fords and ferries, for the building of a bridge may point to the upkeep or improvement of a road for wheeled traffic. Where we still have surviving such a feature as the Brig o' Balgownie (fig. 26) which is wide enough to take vehicles, we are entitled to give at least the benefit of the doubt to those who would argue that before the death of Robert I a genuine road led northward from Old Aberdeen across the River Don.[4]

In fact, we have references to roads and highways almost as soon as we have record material. King David I, staying on one occasion at Staplegordon, that delightful spot in Upper Eskdale, and wishful to protect the hunting rights of Robert Bruce in Annandale, commanded travellers to keep to the *recta via nominata,* perhaps only a bridleway but clearly a permanent and definable route, conceivably signposted.[5] An ancient road in Berwickshire, running across the country from Bunkle towards Oldhamstocks, seems to be referred to in another of King David's charters under the name of 'Crhachoctrestrete'.[6] Again, we cannot be sure from the documents that this was a vehicle road, though the fact that it was called a *strata* makes it likely that we are dealing with a genuine or supposed Roman road, not a mere footpath. In less out of the way parts we hear a good deal of the 'high road' (*magna strata, magna via*), the 'king's highway' (*via regia, via regis*), the 'public' or 'common' highway (*publica via, communis via, communis strata*).[7] Often these public roads are identified by destinations which are well-known royal or baronial burghs. Thus, we have 'the king's highway which leads to Forfar',[8] 'the public road which leads as far as the town of Perth',[9] 'the king's highway reaching towards Roxburgh',[10] 'my royal road which goes from Forres towards Elgin',[11] 'the road coming from Berwick upon Tweed to Haddington bridge',[12] 'the king's highway coming from Lauder',[13] etc.

Here I doubt if we are dealing with tracks fit only for foot passengers and packhorses. In 1138 King David employed many engines for the siege of Wark on Tweed, withdrawing them when the siege proved fruitless.[14] At one point the garrison made a sortie and captured the Scots' provision wagons passing to and fro. Were these siege-engines and wagons built on the spot only for use in the immediate vicinity? Surely not. A generation later the king envisaged that fish would be brought to Kelso in cartloads, presumably all the way from the sea, and that goods of all kinds loaded upon carts would be converging on Roxburgh market from many directions.[15] At the same period the lepers of St Andrews had a cart going when needed to the King's Muir of Crail to fetch whins and heath.[16]

When Edward I embarked upon the conquest of Scotland in 1296 he found a road system not inadequate for his purpose. Occasionally we hear of money being spent on repairing or rebuilding a road, or even making an entirely new roadway, but the rarity of such references suggests that English armies with their heavy baggage trains and siege-engines were able to make use of the roads they found. Most of the Scottish expeditions of Edward I and his son and grandson chose the east coast route into Scotland, despite the greater mileage involved. This, I believe, was because a well-tried road system through relatively flat Northumberland and Durham connected, by the famous bridge at Berwick and by other crossings of the Tweed at Norham, Coldstream and Sprouston, with a reasonably good road system in the Tweed valley and Lothian. On the west side the high road through Lancashire had to negotiate the Shap-Howgill barrier, and the high road from Yorkshire had to cross Stainmore. Any sizeable army or baggage train had then to negotiate the fords of Solway north-west of Carlisle, and would still be faced by a choice of difficult routes through upper Nithsdale or upper Annandale.

During the Edwardian wars in Scotland very large quantities of supplies and munitions were transported by road, some by packhorse but much by means of horse-drawn carts (*carectae*) and ox-wagons (*plaustra*). Journey times could be impressively short. For example, wages money was conveyed from York to Stirling in the summer of 1304 in two carts each pulled by five horses, taking only seven days, a rate of over 30 miles a day.[17] In the same period weapons were carried from London to Stirling in three carts which took sixteen days and from Lincoln to Stirling in one cart taking ten days.[18] At least 83 miles of these journeys were over Scottish high roads. Almost certainly much use was made of the king's highway which ran from Roxburgh to Edinburgh by way of Lauderdale and Soutra, following for many miles the general route and sometimes the actual line of the great Agricolan road from Corbridge to Cramond and Inveresk — Dere Street (see Maxwell, figs. 17–18) as it had come to be called in Anglo-Saxon times. Again and again in charters of the twelfth and thirteenth centuries we can pick up stretches of this major traffic route in contexts which make it most improbable that the clerks had in mind no more than a rude and fluctuating track. Between Dalkeith and Ford 'the king's highway called Derestrete' formed a permanent estate and parish boundary.[19] Near Soutra and south of Lauder tributary by-roads led into 'the king's highway running towards Roxburgh'.[20] This was the road traversed by Edward I's great army of 1298 on its way to Falkirk, and this was also the road traversed by Edward II's great army on its way to Bannockburn. It will be recalled that the well-informed author of the *Life of Edward II* says of that army's baggage wagons that if they had been lined up together they would have stretched for twenty miles.[21] We may assume that the army, which took six days to reach Falkirk from the Tweed, moved faster than its supply wagons—but not much faster, since a good deal of the baggage got through to Bannockburn, implying a rate of progress of eleven or twelve miles a day. In view of the traffic congestion which must surely have prevailed, this does not seem a bad average and is certainly compatible only with a road fit for the passage of wheeled vehicles.

The record of Edward I's wars also gives evidence of what we may call 'awkward' or 'wide' loads. Siege-engines were naturally transported by sea whenever this was possible, but, where it was not, roads were or could be made to serve. An engine was carried from Linlithgow to Queensferry in 1303,[22] and in the following year a large engine was carried from Linlithgow to Stirling on 21 carts.[23] For the siege of Bothwell in 1302 an engine called 'Le Berefrey' was transported from Glasgow on thirty carts in two days.[24] Road haulage was also used for food, drink and exotic luxuries. When King Edward I wintered at Dunfermline in 1303–1304 an iron-bound cart covered with boards and suitable for holding bread was provided to carry the royal household's bread supplies.[25] At Traquair the English king's butlery employed a 'long cart'.[26] The Prince of Wales, it seems, could not campaign in Scotland without his lion, which travelled in a special cart and enjoyed its own commissariat arrangements.[27]

By carefully piecing together the surviving fragments of charter evidence as R.P. Hardie did for the medieval roads of Lauderdale,[28] we may one day be able to construct a reasonably complete network of Scottish main roads used from the twelfth to the fourteenth century, after which time it is possible that deterioration set in. Such a network would evidently include main roads linking Berwick upon Tweed with Haddington and Roxburgh and also a main road from Roxburgh to Edinburgh. There seems to have been a carriage road of some sort in the upper Tweed valley, probably linking Selkirk with Peebles and then running westward, presumably to join another main road in upper Clydesdale. Edward I was able to have materials for the new pele of Selkirk, stones, timber and iron, transported in 1301–2 by wagons, carts and horses.[29] In the 1290s Simon Fraser of Oliver Castle conceded a right of passage for the ox-wagons and horse-carts of Melrose Abbey over a road which led through his lands of Happrew to the king's highway in the land of Edston above Neidpath.[30] This was surely done so that the monks of Melrose could get their loads on to a main traffic artery, either down the Tweed to their abbey or perhaps northward to a market such as Edinburgh or seaport such as Leith.

Our network would safely include a main road (*magna via*) running south-west from Edinburgh to Biggar, more or less on the line of the present A702. At West Linton in the twelfth century this road crossed the Lyne Water by the significantly named 'Biggeresford'.[31] It was surely the existence of this good east-west road which enabled John Comyn of Badenoch and Simon Fraser, who would both know it well, to carry out their bold surprise attack on John Segrave's force at Roslin in February, 1303. The achievement of surprise was due to the Scots' being able to ride through the night from Biggar, nearly thirty miles away.[32] It was evidently by this same road that Edward I in the aftermath of Falkirk had journeyed across country from Glencorse to Ayr.[33] In 1296 Hugh Cressingham actually required the entire Scottish wool clip to be brought to Berwick for export, so that the English 'maltolt' of 40s per sack might be more easily levied upon it.[34] Wool, of course, was often carried on the backs of packhorses, and we should also bear in mind that Cressingham's decree excited a protest from the burgesses of Ayr. But it is at least worth considering that so ambitious a scheme of economic centralisation was founded upon a knowledge that the Scottish road system would prove adequate for the task, and that at least a part of all this wool was intended to reach Berwick in wheeled vehicles.

North of the Forth the provision of main roads may have been markedly inferior, but main roads undoubtedly existed. On the south coast of Fife the main road from Durie in Scoonie (near Leven) to St Ford in Kilconquhar apparently took its course 'along the sands'.[35] The fact that so many of Fife's chief inhabited places were on the coast and the evident importance of the Queensferry, the Earl's Ferry—i.e. the earl of Fife's ferry across to North Berwick—and the earl of Angus's ferry from Tayport to Broughty, suggest that much if not most of Fife's traffic was seaborne. The

Queensferry was so called because Queen Margaret (d. 1093) made it free for *bona fide* pilgrims travelling to St Andrews. This fact gives special interest to the reference in a hitherto unknown fourteenth century charter, dating before 1327, to a 'public road called in English Pilgrymgath ['pilgrims' way']' in the south of Ceres parish.[36] Pilgrim traffic may also have been involved in the reference by Roger bishop of St Andrews (1198–1202) to the 'three ancient and customary exits' from the city of St Andrews in a charter belonging to the close of the twelfth century.[37] There were certainly main roads across Fife,[38] as certainly there were through Strathearn and Strathmore. There was even a main road, though a poor one, carried with obvious difficulty over ill-maintained causeways, over the boggy Cowie Mounth between Stonehaven and Deeside.[39]

Some Angus documents of the thirteenth century introduce us to gradations of quality among available roads. For example, among the marches of Dunnichen we hear of the 'king's highway', the 'Fishergait' and the 'white way' (*alba via*).[40] In the upland parish of Kingoldrum on the edge of the Highland line we see a distinction drawn between a 'common way' (*communis via*) and a 'Scottish way' (*via Scoticana*).[41] In records of this period 'Scottish' means 'pertaining to Gaelic-speaking Scotland north of Forth', more particularly to the older order of things in that region before the advent of Anglo-Norman innovation. It would perhaps not be rash to think of a *via Scoticana* as the sort of road familiar in the Highlands before the days of George Wade. Yet there was undoubtedly an expectation of wheeled traffic in the north in King Robert I's grant to the monks of Arbroath of free ish and entry in the royal forest of Drum 'for transporting their timber with ox-wagons, carts and horses and any other method preferred'.[42]

Bridges are well in evidence north of Forth. Many of them may have been narrow affairs, largely or wholly built of timber. Contemporary accounts of the narrowness of Stirling Bridge in 1297 are well known. A name such as *Stanbrig* for a passage of the Luther Water in the Mearns at least suggests a structure of some permanence.[43] The Brig o' Balgownie has been noticed already. Although less well-known than Bishop Cheyne's *magnum opus*, because it has long since disappeared, the bridge which in the thirteenth century spanned the River Spey a few miles below Rothes must have represented quite as notable an achievement in its way.[44] Much care and local wealth were evidently devoted to the *pons de Spee*, and in later, less happy times its memory was preserved by the fact that the ferry which had to take its place was called the Boat of Brig.[45] Occasionally a landowner might hope to get his road improvement done on the cheap. Sir John Comyn, father of the victor of Roslin, granted passage to the Augustinian canons of Inchaffray, for their animals, wheeled vehicles and goods, through his wood of Rosmadirdyne, provided that they would build and maintain at their own expense a bridge on Sir John's land at the 'black ford' or, as it was called in Gaelic, 'ford of the birch wood' (*athebethy*).[46] The canons were graciously permitted to use this bridge in perpetuity without Sir John or his heirs imposing any charge. We hear elsewhere of Inchaffray Abbey's wagons and other load-bearing vehicles (*vecturae*) used for the transport of building stone from the quarry at Gascon Hall.[47]

The case for a genuine road system in medieval Scotland scarcely needs further labouring, although that system still requires to be worked out in detail, and it would be especially valuable to have some clear evidence of when it was at its height and when it began to decline, if decline it did.

A second feature of the utmost interest is the extent to which this medieval system may have had its origins in the road pattern established by the Romans from the governorship of Agricola, towards the end of the first century, to the reign of Septimius Severus in the first decade of the third century. In spite of the extensive work of archaeologists during the past thirty or forty years it may be doubted whether the historical importance of the Roman road system in Scotland has penetrated the popular consciousness. It still seems to be the general belief that Roman route-finding and road-building constituted a merely ephemeral episode soon giving way to a lengthy dark-age and medieval period in which any earlier roads were forgotten and no new ones were constructed.

Besides the considerable evidence for the survival of long sections of Dere Street, already touched upon, we may note that the ancient and now lost Berwickshire road known in the twelfth century as 'Crhachoctrestrete'[48] may have represented the road which the Romans may be presumed to have built between Berwick and East Lothian.[49] In this connection we need to take into account not only the alignments of a few local minor roads and farm roads but also the place-name Causewaybank (N.G.R., NT 877590). All occurrences of the Old English word *straet* (Middle English, *strete*) in medieval documents should be examined carefully to see whether, in their context, they indicate the possible—or believed—existence of Roman paved roads. Similar elements, e.g. O.E. *stan,* 'stone', especially when combined with 'ford', and forms for causeway, e.g. *calcei-a,-um, chaucee, calsay* etc., should likewise be looked at for the same purpose.

Thus, in a charter of William I of the 1160s or '70s a highway south of Stirling, very likely to be on the line of the Agricolan road from Camelon to Ardoch by way of the Fords of Drip, is described as the '*magna strata* running to Cuiltedouenald'.[50] An undoubted stretch of this same Roman road further north, between Strageath and 'Bertha', well described in Margary's survey,[51] was said in the seventeenth century to be known as 'the street way', 'because it runs in a straight line for the most part, and is cassied with stone . . . and is said to be done either by the Picts or the Romans'.[52] On General Roy's map of 1750 the spot where the road from Cupar in Fife to Kilmany crosses the Moonzie Burn (N.G.R., NO 381179) is marked as Streetford. This name, now obsolete, appears on the earliest Ordnance Survey six-inch map (1854) and although no longer in use is still remembered today by older inhabitants in the district.[53]

In view of the late Sir Ian Richmond's remarkable discovery of the Roman road built west-east across Craik Moor and over Craik Cross Hill from Raeburnfoot in Eskdale (ultimately from Lockerbie) towards Newstead near Melrose[54] it is worth drawing attention to the fact that a crossing of the Ale Water near Satchels in the parish of Lilliesleaf, Roxburghshire was known in the twelfth and thirteenth centuries as 'Staniford'.[55] This crossing, at approximately N.G.R., NT 500233, appears to be on a line drawn straight across country from the north-eastern extremity of the Craik Cross section unearthed by Richmond to the Roman fort at Newstead. The alignment proposed by R.P. Hardie,[56] a good deal further south, would bring the eastern end of this road to join Dere Street at a point on Ancrum Moor about five miles south of Newstead. This line may perhaps be thought preferable in view of the nature of the terrain. Nevertheless, the location and character of 'Staniford' would be worth serious archaeological investigation.

On the other hand, even although the Middle Ages did possess a road system, probably founded on the Roman system, it would obviously be wrong to give the impression that Scottish land communications were ever easy in the medieval period or that they chiefly took the form of carriage roads. To get the perspective right we should do well to heed the immemorial formula of the old charters, *in viis et semitis*, 'in ways and paths'.[57] The geography of Scotland, with its hill ranges often lying across the grain of the country as it were, its fast rivers of uncertain temper, its fearful mosses and bogs, its many arms of the sea running far inland, has at all times imposed upon human communication a complex pattern of routes by land and water. Something of this pattern may be discerned in the famous fourteenth century map of Britain preserved among the Gough MSS in the Bodleian Library.[58] Although the map is perhaps as late as *c.* 1350–60, its noticeably imperfect Scottish information was probably somewhat out of date, and may well represent the situation nearer the reign of Robert I. The most remarkable feature of the MS is that for South Britain it is essentially a road map, with both roads and mileages shown. North of Hadrian's Wall no roads or mileages are attempted, but this is certainly not because no roads existed.[59] It is possible to argue that even for North Britain the Gough Map was still meant to serve travellers, for it features bridges, fords, ferries and passes as well as obvious travellers' destinations such as burghs, castles and monasteries. But this aspect ought not to be exaggerated, for the truth seems to be that the Scottish information contained on the map is scarcely more than the minimum to be expected in a work of this scale and evident ambition. Even then some of this information—e.g. the configuration of the coastline of northern Scotland—is seriously misleading. Yet we can, I believe, trace a few major routes and one or two minor ones. One leads from Berwick and Roxburgh, by Lauder and Soutra, to Edinburgh. A Clyde Valley route includes Crawford, Lanark, Bothwell, Rutherglen, Glasgow and Dumbarton. A Strathmore route leads northward from Perth to Aberdeen by way of Coupar Angus, Glamis, Forfar, Brechin, Inverbervie and Cowie near Stonehaven. Certain crucial communication links are shown, among them the Fords of Solway; the Queensferry; the fords of Drip above Stirling; the *pons Aghmore* which, though marked as being in Menteith, I would take to be Auchmuir Bridge, just east of Loch Leven; the bridge of Perth; and two passes through the eastern Grampians, the Capell Mounth and the Cowie Mounth.

It is worthwhile digressing for a moment to deal with the identity of *pons Aghmore*, if only to try to clear up a confusion. The names 'Aghmore' (Gough Map) and Auchmuir (Fife) both represent Gaelic *àth mór*, 'big ford'. Auchmuir first occurs in a record of the early twelfth century as 'Admore', when the place was given to the *célidé* (culdees) of Loch Leven by Ethelred, brother of the kings Edgar, Alexander I and David I.[60] A bridge, evidently over the River Leven, existed before 1159,[61] and in view of the probability that Auchmuir was the highest point below the river's exit from Loch Leven at which it could be forded or bridged conveniently it seems that this twelfth century bridge was in fact at the site of Auchmuir Bridge. Since this would have been an essential link in a line of communication running north-south between Perth or at least Bridge of Earn and the West Fife termini of various crossings of the Forth, it further seems likely that the Gough mapmaker would have intended to include Auchmuir Bridge on his map and that his *pons Aghmore* was meant to indicate this feature.

But we know from the topographical data embodied in an early chapter of Walter Bower's expanded *Scotichronicon*[62] that there was a ford in Menteith, evidently of some importance, known as Auchmore, 'big ford'. Bower lists Auchmore immediately after Arnprior and 'Louch Gartur'. The latter feature is presumably what is now shown on the Ordnance Survey one-inch map as Black Loch, a bog between Gartur and the Loch of Inchmahome ('Lake of Menteith'). It would appear that Bower's Auchmore was a ford across the River Forth at Cardross, an ancient estate whose lands occupy an island of higher ground in the midst of what until comparatively recent times must have been almost impassable morass. If this 'big ford' was well known to travellers it could have come to the notice of the Gough mapmaker and led him, erroneously, to place his *pons Aghmore* in Menteith.

One or two of the Gough Map's place-names are worth pondering if we seek to push our study of routes back beyond the time of record. Solway, *súl vath*, 'pillar ford', reminds us of such names as Stakeford in Northumberland, the Tay fishery at Perth called 'Stoc' or 'le Stok',[63] probably on the line of an ancient ford, and the 'Stockford' which Andrew Wyntoun preserves as the name of the ford across the Beauly River between Lovat and Beauly.[64] Fords secured by means of wooden stakes and tree trunks are a very ancient device for aiding human travel. The Queensferry explains itself, although now that it is several years since we have had a road as well as a rail crossing of the Forth from Dalmeny to Inverkeithing I suppose we may be in danger of forgetting the one great benefaction of Saint Margaret to the Scottish nation whose importance is hardly controversial. *Pons Aghmore* reminds us to look for fords when we find bridges and *vice versa*. 'Nechtan's ford', *àth Neachtain*, now Naughton in Balmerino,[65] marked the crossing of the burn which flows from Newton to the Motray Water in north-east Fife. Saint Maelrubha's ford, preserved as Amulree, must have been an important and at times difficult passage over the Perthshire River Braan. Almost any old land perambulation that has survived in record will demonstrate the wellnigh obsessive interest which our ancestors took in fords, many of them marking the most convenient place at which to cross what seem to us to be quite inconsiderable watercourses. The marches of Kingoldrum in Angus, as described in the middle of the thirteenth century,[66] take us in turn to the ford of 'Dersy', the burn ford of 'Aqhkragy', now Ascreavie, a certain ford called 'Madzor', and a ford over the Carity Burn called Auchnahilt. It is hard for us in these days of instant bridges and almost instant cattle-grids to imagine ourselves back into a time when even a small burn in spate might be impassable and when a knowledge of the firmest crossing places was essential for everyone in the community. It would not be an exaggeration to say that the medieval pattern of roads and routes was very largely determined by the position of the most favoured fording places, so that an apparently erratic or roundabout route may prove on examination to have been perfectly sensible. Crossing places, whether by ford, bridge or ferry, have left many traces on the modern map. The 'Boats' on the Spey, such as Boat of Brig, Blacks Boat, Boat of Garten and Boat of Insh, are well known. The earliest Spey ferry on record was that operated at Fochabers in the thirteenth century by Dougal the ferryman, who had two boats.[67] The Coble of Dalreoch was where the Auchterarder-Perth road crossed the Earn, some miles down river from the Roman ford at Strageath.[68] The *batellum passagii de Munros*, or 'fery bait of Montros', taking travellers over the South Esk beside Rossie Island, was a valuable property of Arbroath Abbey.[69] Ford in North Northumberland, at a passing place over the treacherous Till, and Ford in Midlothian, where Dere Street crossed the Scottish Tyne, are both old-established names, the former being a place of parochial status.

Oxenfoord likewise is an early name. Birgham on the Tweed, an apparently ancient name meaning 'bridge settlement', poses a real puzzle, for there is scarcely even a rivulet in the place to be bridged; yet to imagine a bridge across the Tweed in early Northumbrian times seems to verge on fantasy.

Penpont in Dumfriesshire is pure Cumbric for 'Bridgend', to be compared on the one hand with the Welsh place-names Bridgend in Glamorgan and Talybont, literally 'forehead of the bridge', and on the other hand with Penrith in Cumberland, *pen rhyd*, 'end of the ford'. In King Malcolm IV's charter of 1161 confirming his stewardship to Walter son of Alan, the king also confirms to Walter the lands of Renfrew and its dependencies.[70] Between Pollok and Cathcart was an unidentified 'Talahret'. In a letter written not long before his death, the late Professor Melville Richards agreed with my suggestion that this might possibly represent Welsh *tal y rhyd*, 'head or end of the ford', in which case we should probably look for an old crossing of the White Cart Water, perhaps in the district of Langside. The farm names of Auchendavy in Kirkintilloch and Auchinstarry, by Croy in Cumbernauld, are of special interest among names for river crossings. The former appears to represent *áth nan damh*, 'oxen ford' (compare Oxenfoord in Midlothian) or, in the singular, *àth an daimh*, 'ox's ford'. The place is marked by an Antonine Wall fort. The second certainly stands for *àth na staire*, 'ford of the causeway' or 'stepping stones'. Both place-names may ultimately go back, behind their Q-Celtic forms, to P-Celtic names indicating crossings of the River Kelvin used in the period of Roman occupation.

Kindrochit, now Braemar, tells of an early bridge over the Clunie Water, Kindrought east of Strichen of another over the North Ugie. Pitpointie in Auchterhouse[71] seems to indicate a bridge already in existence before Pictish name-forming habits had died out—perhaps a bridge across a bog rather than a definite watercourse. An old Gaelic word for a water crossing apparently of the stepping-stone or rough bridge type was *stair*, related to modern Gaelic *tarsuinn*, Welsh *traws*, 'across'. From *stair* we have the lost St Andrews name Kinnastare,[72] 'end of the crossing', 'causeyend' or 'causeyhead'; and also the Nairnshire name Kinstearie.[73] It has given rise to another St Andrews name, Stermolind, 'crossing by the mill', evidently upgraded by the twelfth century when we have the first mention of the Stermolind Brig,[74] which carried the road eastward from St

Andrews over the Kinness Burn. There are also, of course, the simplex Starr in north-east Fife on the Motray Water, Starr of Markinch (also Fife, at a difficult crossing of a still undrained bog) and Stair in Ayrshire at what looks to be an early crossing place over the River Ayr. A rather later word for stepping stones was *clacharan*, preserved in such names as Clattering Brig and Clatternford.[75]

To the steep and often difficult slope by which a road or track had to descend to or ascend from a ford or bridge the Old English language gave the name *peth* or *path*, found very widely in Northumbria, where indeed it is still a living word, if only just. In Scotland *peth* forms a not uncommon element in place-names, usually with the vowel opened to 'a'. Cockburnspath, *Colbrandes peth*,[76] is where the Berwick-Dunbar road negotiated the ravine of the Dunglass Burn, Hexpath is where the A697 until very recently corkscrewed its way across the ravine and bog formed by a little tributary of the Eden Water.[77] Pathhead is at the top of the steep slope to the Tyne at Ford. Neidpath is where the A72 route finds its way—still with some difficulty—through the narrow ravine of the Tweed west of Peebles. One Redpath is on a steep slope overlooking the Whiteadder Water, another by a steep-sided tributary valley of the Leader Water in Earlston. A surprisingly northerly example is the twelfth century 'Crospath' in Fordoun, which has evidently been Gaelicised and then re-anglicised as Corsebauld.[78] The true Gaelic equivalent of *peth* was *claon*, a slope or declivity, found in the tautologous Clune Brae above Port Glasgow and the similarly named slope which takes the road from the head of Glen Urquhart down into Strathglass. An exact counterpart of Pathhead is Kinclune in Kingoldrum. Clunie, often meaning 'the place at the *peth*', is of course a common name.[79]

Passes or defiles constituted a still more serious obstacle for the traveller than peths, even though they were often his only means of avoiding still greater obstacles. The Highlands naturally abounded in passes, to every one of which a name has no doubt been given at one time or another. The commonest Gaelic words for pass, *larig* and *bealach*, are still in current use, and are also embedded in long established place-names such as Finlarig, Perthshire, Dillars in Lesmahagow, Lanarkshire and Doularg, Ayrshire, all containing *larig*, and Balloch on Loch Lomond and Ballo near Abernethy (denoting a small pass through the Ochils), representing *bealach*.

The Fife place-name Glen Vale, referring to the deep gap between the West Lomond and Bishop Hill, embodies *bealach* in the genitive (*gleann a' bhealaich*), while the nominative still appears in the name of Ballo Farm at the head of this 'pass'. Another word for pass, common in the Lowlands, was 'cross' or 'Corse', apparently identical with the Gaelic word *crasg*, a crossing place. This word is found in Glencorse, Corsincan near Blyth Bridge, in Crosscryne near Biggar, and Corsencon in New Cumnock, all passes and boundary points in Midlothian, Peeblesshire, Lanarkshire and Ayrshire respectively. The word is also involved in the nice piece of Buchan tautology, Corse of Balloch, by which a route seems once to have gone through the peat mosses between Hatton and Kinmundy.

References

1. Fairhurst, H., 'The Roads of Scotland. I. Roman Roads', *Scottish Geographical Magazine,* **71** (1955), 77–82; Moir, D.G., 'The Roads of Scotland. II. Statute Labour Roads', *ibid.,* **73** (1957), 101–110.
2. *Ibid.,* p. 101.
3. *OSA* (*Old Statistical Account*), **16** (1795), 73.
4. For the Brig o' Balgownie or Bridge of Don see, *inter alia, Aberdeen Registrum,* **1,** 227; *Aberdeen-Banff Coll.,* 79, 155 (before 1308?).
5. Lawrie, *Charters,* no. 199. Probably the 'naming' of this road formed part of forest regulations designed to prevent poaching by establishing 'prohibited roads' (*forisvie*), for which see *Melrose Liber,* no. 39 and *APS,* **1,** 687, cap. viii and especially cap. ix.
6. *RND,* nos. 14 ('Crachoctre'), 36 [= *RRS,* **2,** no. 181, q.v. for comment] ('Crhachoctrestrete'), 168 ('Cracocketrestrete'). The name is now lost but appears to mean 'Roman [or paved] road by the oak tree frequented by crakes'. Its location may be determined by reference to the other boundary points specified, from which it may be inferred that it ran north-west of Billie in a north-westerly direction to a ford over the Eye Water at N.G.R., NT 799638. The parish boundary between Bunkle and Coldingham from Billie to this point runs along the course of a burn which may be the 'Mereburne' ('march burn') of the charters, thence across open country until it joins a road leading to the ford. This ford is possibly the one referred to as 'Halyford' in 1431 (*RND,* no. 639).
7. See, e.g., *RRS,* **1** and **2,** Index of Subjects, s.vv. 'highway', 'road', 'street'. To these references may be added a 13th century mention of both minor roads and the 'King's highway' at Falkirk, the latter presumably representing the Agricolan road from Falkirk to Stirling (SRO (Scottish Record Office), Reg. Ho. chrs., no. 17).

8. *Arbroath Liber,* **1,** no. 232 (13th–14th cent. ?).
9. *Inchaffray Chrs.*, no. 108 (1278).
10. *RRS,* **1,** no. 216 (1162–4).
11. *Ibid.,* **2,** no. 159 (1176?).
12. *Ibid.,* no. 459 (1205–7).
13. *Dryburgh Liber,* 267 (*c.* 1170–80). Compare the 'royal highway' [also 'great highway'] leading from Loch Lomond towards Dumbarton, *Paisley Registrum,* 212, 215.
14. Anderson, *Early Sources,* **2,** 188, 208.
15. *RRS,* **2,** no 64.
16. *Ibid.*, no. 370 (*c.* 1195).
17. *Cal. Docs. Scot.,* **4,** 461–2.
18. *Ibid.,* 462–3.
19. *RRS,* **1,** no. 236. This section is of course the route of a modern road passing through the significantly named Chesterhill. For Dere Street in Scotland, see Margary, I.D., *Roman Roads in Britain* (rev. edn., 1967), 484–8; *RCAMS* (Roxburgh), **2,** 463–74; Hardie, R.P., *The Roads of Medieval Lauderdale* (1942), 23–103, especially 67, 88, 98–9.
20. *RRS,* **1,** no. 216; **2,** no. 236.
21. *Vita Edwardi secundi monachi cuiusdam Malmesburiensis,* ed. N. Denholm Young (1957), 50.
22. *Cal. Docs. Scot.,* **4,** 461.
23. *Ibid.,* 467.
24. *Ibid.,* 450.
25. *Ibid.,* 460.
26. *Ibid.,* 465.
27. *Ibid.,* **2,** 364. Cf. *ibid.,* 368 for the loan to Edward I by English religious houses of numerous horses and carts for use in Scottish campaigns.
28. Hardie, *op. cit.* (above, n. 19).
29. *Cal. Docs. Scot.,* **4,** 469.
30. *Melrose Liber,* no. 356 (possibly a road on the line of the Roman road designated 79a by Margary, *Roman Roads,* 473–4).
31. *RRS,* **2,** no. 194; cf. Margary, *Roman Roads,* 467–9.
32. Barrow, G.W.S., *Robert Bruce and the Community of the Realm of Scotland* (2nd edn., 1976), 178.
33. Gough, H., *Itinerary of Edward I,* **2,** 168–9. No place of issue is listed between Glencorse and Ayr.
34. Barrow, *Robert Bruce,* 110 and n. 7.
35. *Cal. Docs. Scot.,* **4,** 474.
36. St Andrews University Library, MS 37490/1 (Collairnie charters). I owe this reference to the kindness of Mr R.N. Smart.
37. SRO, MS 'Black Book' of St Andrews, fo. 35, presumably referring

to the North Gait, South Gait and the road south over the 'Stermolind brig' leading to Anstruther and Crail.

38. For roads in the Kirkcaldy-Leven area in the later 13th century, see Fraser, *Wemyss,* **2,** no. 2.

39. J. Craig Watt, *The Mearns of Old* (1914), 156–61.

40. *Arbroath Liber,* **1,** no. 232 (13th–14th cent. ?).

41. British Library, MS. Add. 33245, f. 179^{v}.

42. *Arbroath Liber,* **1,** no. 284. Note also that there was a wagon road (*via quadrigarum*) in the royal forest south of Banff, in the area denoted by the modern estate of Park of Cornhill, in 1242 (*Aberdeen-Banff Illustrations*, 109). Note also the striking statement in *Macfarlane's Geographical Collections,* **2,** 598: 'Ther is a way from the yate of Blair in Athoil to Ruffen in Badenoch maid by David Cuming Earle of Athoill for carts to pass with wyne, and the way is called Rad-na-pheny or way of wane wheills, it is layd with calsay in sundrie parts'. Rad-na-pheny would stand for *rathad fiona* (or *an fhiona*), 'road of the wine'. Earl David 'Cuming' would probably have been the 13th century Earl David Hastings (1244–7) rather than the 14th century Earl David of Strathbogie (1307–26, forfeited 1314).

43. *Arbroath Liber,* **1,** no. 144. The same record mentions the 'bridge of Luffenoct', evidently spanning the Luthnot Burn in Marykirk (formerly Aberluthnot), now perhaps the Burn of Balmakelly. Note also a stone bridge across a burn at Inverallan by Grantown on Spey in the 13th century (*Moray Registrum*, no. 128).

44. *Moray Registrum*, nos. 106–13.

45. Subsequently, of course, the boat was replaced by a bridge. For other boats on the Spey see below. For the eighteen boats across the River Dee and fourteen across the River Don in 1732 see *Aberdeen-Banff Collections*, 77.

46. *Inchaffray Chrs.,* no. 108.

47. *Ibid.,* no. 95 (1266).

48. Above, and n. 6.

49. Note Margary's words anent the Devil's Causeway in North Northumberland: 'it continued *at least* to Berwick' (*Roman Roads*, 480, my italics).

50. *RRS,* **2,** no. 130 (p. 207).

51. Margary, *Roman Roads*, 493–5.

52. *Macfarlane's Geographical Collections,* **1,** 133.

53. Ex inf. Lt.-Col. T.L. Rollo, Brackland, Cupar.

54. Margary, *Roman Roads,* 461–4; *PSAS,* **80** (1945–6), 103–17.

55. *Glasgow Registrum,* **1,** no. 99. (p. 85). Compare *RRS,* **2,** no. 215, where 'Staniford' appears to refer to the same place, in the vicinity of Synton Mill. Note also that a crossing of the burn which descends

eastward from above Ballingry in West Fife was called 'the stanry ffurde of Navathy [Navitie]', in the 15th century (*St Andrews Liber*, 1); and compare Stanneryhaugh in Fettercairn, Kincardineshire (N.G.R., No. 692744).

56. Margary, *Roman Roads*, 464.

57. A footpath (*semita peditum*) might be clearly distinguished, e.g. that provided for the local laird and his family to go from his house to St Quivox kirk near Ayr (*Paisley Reg.*, 228).

58. I have used the edition of E.J.S. Parsons (Royal Geographical Society and Bodleian Library, 1958).

59. The statement by Parsons (*op. cit.*, 12) that 'No road pattern exists north of Hadrian's Wall' refers to the Gough map itself, not to medieval actuality.

60. Lawrie, *Charters,* no. 14 (p. 11; cf. pp. 243, 245).

61. *Ibid.,* no. 263.

62. *Chron. Bower,* **1,** 46.

63. *Arbroath Liber,* nos. 6, 100 (p. 71).

64. *Chron. Wyntoun* (Laing), **2,** 174 (Bk. VII, c. v), 'Stokfurd'.

65. *St Andrews Liber,* 107 (and numerous other references); *RRS,* **1,** no. 228.

66. BL, MS. Add. 33245, ff. 179–80.

67. *Cal. Docs. Scot,* **4,** 375.

68. See the map in *Inchaffray Chrs.,* facing 316.

69. *Arbroath Liber,* **1,** no. 9; **2,** no. 447 ('fery bait of Montros'); *Retours* (Forfar), nos. 154 ('lie boittis passage de Monros'), 384 (*cymba portatoria de Montrose*).

70. *RRS,* **1,** no. 184.

71. *St Andrews Liber,* 284, 325; a wholly P-Celtic name.

72. *Ibid.,* 122 (and numerous other references).

73. Compare Auchinstarry in Cumbernauld, already mentioned.

74. *Ibid.,* 127 (and other references).

75. On *stair* and *clacharan*, see Watson, *CPNS,* 200; RIA, *Contributions to a Dictionary of the Irish Language,* s.v. *clochrán*; E. Hogan, *Onomasticon Goedelicum,* s.v. *clochrán*; Watt, *The Mearns of Old,* 322.

76. Lawrie, *Charters,* no. 153 (p. 118)

77. N.G.R., NT 657469.

78. *Arbroath Liber,* **1,** no. 89.

79. In some instances Clunie may be derived from Gaelic *cluain*, fem., 'meadow', 'green plain'; knowledge of the local terrain will usually indicate which word is involved.

Bridges and Roads in Scotland: 1400–1750

Ted Ruddock

My subject is the physical structure of masonry bridges built in Scotland in the years 1400 to 1750, with some comment on the nature of the roads which formed the other component of the land transport routes. As it is based on strictly limited research, the synthesis presented is a tentative one; but unexpected facts have emerged which I hope will lead to more thorough investigation. The bridges which have been studied are listed in Table 1 (pp. 86–88).

Roads

In the preceding account Professor Barrow[1] quotes many references to roads fit for vehicular traffic in the years 1100 to 1400. The strongest evidence for the existence of such roads is the rapid passage of military baggage trains and siege engines over important land routes. On the other hand, it is not disputed that between 1100 and 1750 there were many routes used only by horses or men on foot, and others used chiefly for droves of animals.[2] It is not clear that the vehicle roads deteriorated after 1400. Dissatisfaction with individual roads was recorded at various times between then and 1750,[3] but it may have been purely local and temporary; or it may have been prompted by expectations of improving standards rather than actual deterioration of the roads.

While it is quite certain that there were very few vehicle roads through the central and western Highlands at any time during the three centuries 1400–1700, some of the best evidence of the physical structure of Scottish roads at the end of that era is to be found in the records of military surveyors in the Highland region after 1725.[4] A series of notes written by one surveyor on a rough map of the route from Stirling to Fort William,[5] describing the existing roads and recommending repairs, is worth quoting. The distinctions between a 'cart road' and a 'horse road' and between the parts of the route which were good for use in dry weather only and those which were good in all weather, had probably been familiar to travellers on most routes from the medieval centuries onwards. And there is no reason to believe that the methods of survey and choice of alignment, or the materials used, had changed within the same time.

The notes (but not the map) begin at Edinburgh:

> 'From Edr. to Stirling, and Down [i.e. Doune], to Kilmehug [near Callander], in Monteith is already carte road ... Kilmehug begins the road, which is to be mended...' A few miles further on there is 'one little step in the wood to be filled up with stone and lime and made smooth, It is easily made cart road'. Further on, 'By widening the mouth of Lochlubnig which is easily done ... the loch would run out, so as the low way that is markt [on the plan] the side of the loch would be always draye and good road'. Near Edinkip, 'the road to be viewed ... some ashents and deshents may, by changing the road, and mending other places, make it a carte road'. In Glenogle, there is 'ane aschent of a rysing hill but not high, all dry, no precipice, by viewing it and changing the road a few yards in some places, may saive, a good deal of trouble, I have brought a light two wheel chaise up it'. The next stretch as far as Suie is 'along the side of a hill; all bogs and very bad not worth mending' and a change of route is suggested to make a 'good flat road'. Then follows 'a low flatt road and dry, may easily be made carte road', but it is necessary 'to make the road in Strathfillen not through the plaine; for the water [i.e. river] that goes throw it, alters its course, and is troublesome and oft not passible, the side of the hill just above it is a dry gravellie road already; may easily be made a constant good road and carte road not much up or down...'

This shows that the wisdom of choosing ground with good natural drainage for the line of the road, and if possible with gravelly or stony subsoil, was well understood. Beyond Tyndrum (which is called 'Achinturin') there are alternative routes, one going north by Achallader to Glencoe, which is at first

> 'a rough stonie road no hills, but through dry moors', but further on 'is all moor ... the whole way is forest, no house, much moss and bogs, but by viewing it with guides, and pick out the dryest, may mark out a horse road good in dry weather' to the head of Glencoe, and after Glencoe is 'the Brea of Lochaber, all moorish road, may be viewed and markt out by guides the dryest...'

There is apparently no question of making a cart road here. The alternative route after Tyndrum is

> 'the dry road ... through Glenorchy, Bona[we] Ferrie, and by Appin; is always good, wants a little help in some places. To be viewed and considered: Is but half a day about [i.e. extra journey time]; and both the roads may be made good and good boats to be kept, at those two ferries that are markt'. This route is marked as 'the best winter road to Lochaber'.

Only two bridges existed on the whole route from Kilmahog to Fort William, one over a burn in Glen Dochart and one at Tyndrum. All other crossings of water, even where it was a cart road, must have been by fords, except for the ferries at Bonawe and Ballachulish.

Two inferences can be drawn from these notes. Firstly, a horse road was obtained simply by choosing the best line and marking it; the surface was not made, it was simply that of a beaten track. Secondly, the condition of a cart road was judged by its gradient, roughness and wetness; since causeway is not mentioned, the surface was presumably made and maintained with gravel, stone and lime being used at a few points of special difficulty, which may have been outcrops of rock.

The map and its notes are undated, but other sheets in the same collection[6] bear dates 1724, 1729 and 1735, and all depict the roads and forts proposed or built between 1724 and 1737. The notes may be taken as a description of the route at some time in those years. In 1748–52 the whole road from Stirling to Tyndrum was re-made and extended by the Devil's Staircase route to Fort William,[7] but that was a project of much larger scale than the modest improvements proposed by the earlier surveyor. As no work on the road is mentioned in General Wade's annual reports,[8] it is unlikely that any improvement took place in his time.

Bridges

There can be no doubt that many of the early bridges in Scotland, as in most European countries, were of timber, but lack of surviving examples or clear descriptions makes study of them virtually impossible.

A considerable amount of research on old masonry bridges was done by H.R.G. Inglis in the early years of this century.[9] It appears from his writings that he scanned the published *Acts of the Parliaments of Scotland* (1124–1707), the *Exchequer Rolls* (1264–1600) and *Register of the Privy Council* (1545–1689), as well as some local records. Where other evidence is lacking the dates and, less frequently, dimensions given in his papers are used here without recourse to his apparent sources. He deduced that there was 'an almost total suspension of bridge-building from 1540 to 1570, from 1688 to 1696, and from 1706 to 1720', but otherwise divided the history of bridge-building since 1400 into eight periods distinguished from each other by changes in the chief sources of money.[10] The designated periods were:

(i)	the pre-Reformation period	1400–1560
(ii)	the post-Reformation period	1560–1600
(iii)	the 'collection bridges' period	1600–1680
(iv)	the period of local bridges	1680–1710
(v)	the period of shire and military bridges	1710–1754
(vi)	the turnpike bridges—early period	1754–1770
(vii)	the turnpike bridges–later period	1770–1800
(viii)	the turnpike bridges—heavy or mail-road period	1800–

I shall deal only with the first five of these periods, in which most of the capital funds came from, respectively, (i) the bishops, (ii) the large landowners, (iii) the presbyteries and parishes of the reformed church, with occasional assistance from the General Assembly, (iv) burgh councils and county justices or commissioners of supply raising the money by public subscription, and (v) the same local authorities together with central government.[11] (Some revision of Inglis's framework is probably desirable.)

Many of the oldest bridges in Scotland stand on sites where bridges have existed for many centuries, and most of the surviving structures display evidence of several different stages of construction. Their dates of construction can therefore only be estimated with confidence after detailed study of the existing fabric in conjunction with any available records. Even a date given in an inscription on a bridge can be misleading.[12] Almost all the bridges mentioned here have been subjected to careful examination very recently and there has also been access to some important documents and monographs not known to Inglis, as well as the published *Inventories* of the Royal Commission on the Ancient and Historical Monuments of Scotland. Each date in Table 1 is the best estimate that can be made from all the evidence available. Where no new evidence has been found, Inglis's date[13] has usually been accepted.

Inglis attempted to correlate prominent features and leading dimensions of the surviving bridges[14] with their dates of construction, but several of his conclusions can be questioned. The remainder of the present account is an up-to-date summary of facts concerning the materials, construction methods and leading dimensions of the surviving bridges and a few unexecuted designs. Dates of construction are noted but close relationships between dates and physical features are not generally evident.

Width

The clear width of roadway between parapets determined the amount and type of traffic which a bridge could carry. A width of 8 ft. (2.44 m) was sufficient for a single-wheeled vehicle, except, perhaps, for rare military 'engines'. Two-way traffic required at least 11–12 ft. (3.35–3.66 m). This would be necessary on bridges carrying main routes into large towns and desirable on long bridges even in rural areas.

The original widths of roadway on a random selection of the surviving bridges and on a few unexecuted designs are listed in Table 1. Where the width varies, the minimum width is given. Because some of the bridges have been widened or otherwise altered and their parapets rebuilt, the tabulated widths, based on recent measurements, are subject to minor error, which is unlikely to exceed 1 ft. (0.31 m). The dates are best estimates, from all the available evidence, of those at which the *original* widths of the bridges were established, and written sources of the dates are noted in the final column.

The facts can be summarised as follows:

1. From before 1500 until 1750 bridges which did not carry important roads into large towns were built of various widths from 7½ to 12½ ft. (2.29 to 3.81 m) (only Cramond Brig and Abbey Bridge at Haddington being slightly wider) and there is no evidence of a regular increase of width with the passage of time. In fact, most of the surviving bridges less than 9 ft. (2.74 m) wide are of the 'collection bridge' period and 'collection bridges', being built primarily for access to churches over relatively small rivers,[15] could be made narrower—and also steeper—than bridges for general wheeled traffic.
2. From 1400 to 1725 most bridges carrying important roads into sizeable towns were made 11–14½ ft. (3.35–4.42 m) wide, the only exceptions

being Peebles, 8 ft. (2.44 m) wide, and Berwick Bridge,[16] a special royal project which was 17 ft. (5.18 m) wide. Near the end of the period few bridges were built less than 14 ft. (4.27 m) wide, and greater widths began to be built soon after 1725. On the military roads which were started in 1725, however, 12 ft. (3.66 m) was adopted as a standard width for bridges; these were all on rural roads through the Highlands where the general traffic would always be light, although individual guns or wagons might be large.

An English comparison can be found in the 115 bridges administered by the justices of the West Riding of Yorkshire.[17] They were mostly rural bridges but a small number were at large towns. In 1752 only eight of the 115 were more than 14 ft. (4.27 m) wide and only three more than 16 ft. (4.88 m) wide; eighty-seven were between 7½ and 14 ft. (2.29 m and 4.27 m) wide. Widening of the bridges at the Yorkshire towns began in 1758 and widening of Bridge of Dee and Glasgow Bridge, which occupied similar sites in Scotland, was first considered seriously in the 1770s.[18]

Foundations

Study of the surviving bridges suggests that their builders preferred sites where a single arch could be used with foundations laid on rock above the normal water level. The most obvious examples are Dunblane and Carr Bridges, but there are a number of others at which the foundations are clearly laid on rock which is at or only a few inches below the normal summer water level. Examples are the bridges at Fogo, Burn o' Cambus, Doune (over Ardoch Water), Cleghorn, Mousemill (fig. 27), and the two-arch bridge at East Linton.

In several other instances it appears that the abutments were founded on rock at or above the summer water level but, the river being too wide for a single-arch bridge, piers were founded on rock at a moderate depth below the summer level. Three such bridges are the Bridge of Teith at Doune, built in 1535, North Water Bridge (1539, fig. 28) and the old Avon Bridge at Hamilton, probably also built early in the sixteenth century; a trio near enough both in their dates and type of construction to suggest that there was contact, if not identity, between their builders. Some method must have been devised for lowering the water level while the piers in midstream were founded, and it must be surmised that

Fig. 27. Mousemill Bridge (1649). Hewn-stone arch springing from rock, with rubble spandrels.

Fig. 28. North Water Bridge (1539). Pier founded on rock just below water level.

cofferdams, either of piles (as in fig. 29) or of rammed earth, were used.

This was a common practice in shallow rivers; there is frequent reference to what must have been a cofferdam (though the word

Fig. 29. Cofferdam of wooden piles, with men baling out water (Ramelli, *Le diverse et artificiose machine*, 1588). This was drawn as general illustration of a method, not a particular structure.

used in a translation from Latin is 'bulwark') in the records of the building of a bridge over the Tay at Dunkeld in 1510–16,[19] a little earlier than the three bridges just mentioned. There are several references to supply of logs and boards for the bulwark, one mention of 'workmen labouring at baling water' and another reference to the bulwark 'holding the water from the arch'. Baling by men with scoops and baskets was the common way of lowering the level of water within a cofferdam (see fig. 29), and the dam itself could have been built of logs and boards assembled in several different ways;[20] but whatever the arrangement of timbers, the fixing of its position on the river bed would be most easily accomplished by driving piles, and the use of large numbers of piles to extend the water-excluding wall below the bed should not have presented any difficulty. It is therefore surprising that the word 'piles' occurs only once[21] in the whole record of payments, and the context suggests that what is meant is not piles but whole piers of the bridge. But the surprise extends to two other sixteenth century bridges where excavations have proved the lack of piles, although both stand in tidal rivers. It has been generally thought that piles were indispensable in founding bridge piers in tidal water until at least 1700. The method of 'starlings', described below, made extensive use of piles, and cofferdams high enough to exclude the tide could hardly be built without one or more lines of piles driven to form continuous vertical walls. Moreover, to remove the water which would seep into a cofferdam through the walls and through the river-bed at high tide was generally considered impracticable[22] until hand-driven pumping machines were replaced by steam-driven pumps at the end of the eighteenth century.[23]

One of the two bridges founded without piles was the Bridge of Dee at Aberdeen, built in 1520–27. The old foundations of the piers were examined by William Leslie when he was extending them in 1842 in order to widen the bridge; he described them as follows:[24]

> The masonry stood on frames of oak, as shown [fig. 30], made of timbers 9 to 11 inches diameter, partly flattened on top and bottom, the cross pieces partly checked into the others, and all fixed together by oak pins or dowels. The oak was but little decayed.
>
> There had been no piling or other preparation under the frames, and the frames were from 2 to 5 feet under lowest water ... it appeared to me that the weight of the super-structure had made some of the piers to sink considerably ...

> There was a protective apron, of pitching, of rubble stones, round all the piers, this sprang from a kirb, laid at lowest water, and from 5 to 8 feet distant, and rose up on the piers to about 2 feet above ordinary water level [fig. 30].

The type of frame described had been known in Scotland in previous centuries as a 'brander'[25] and in England was often called a 'grating'. The spacing of the timbers at Bridge of Dee (fig. 30) is much wider than was common in the eighteenth and nineteenth

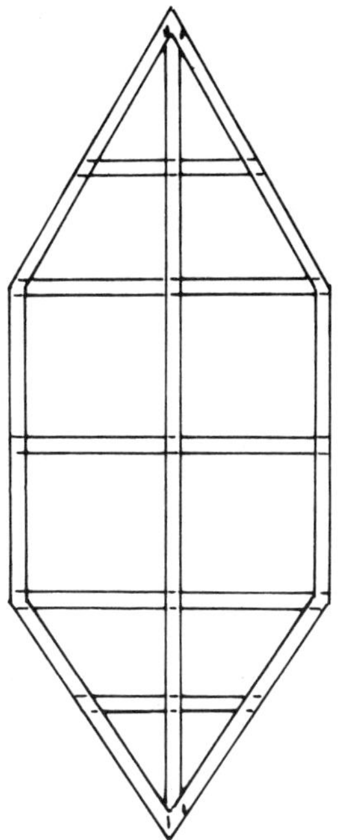

PLAN OF BRANDER

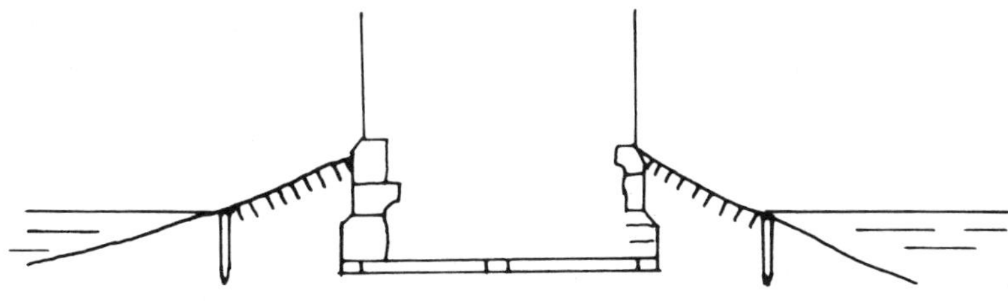

SECTION

Fig. 30. Foundation of a pier of the Bridge of Dee (1527). From Mylne, *Master Masons* (1892).

Fig. 31. Starling at base of a pier of Berwick Bridge (1625). The timber framing at the top of the old starling can be clearly seen; the extra step against the face of the pier is of concrete, and recent. Seaweed covers the stone pitching which lies sloping against the side of the starling and obscures the timber piles which formed the perimeter wall of the starling.

centuries, when the gap between balks was usually only 1–3 ft. (0.31–0.91 m). Protective aprons similar to those described by Leslie can still be seen clearly at Berwick Bridge, but at Berwick they lie against the starlings, not against the piers themselves (fig. 31).

The second bridge founded without piles and examined by excavation is the old Brig of Ayr (fig. 32).[26] A shaft was dug down the middle of each of its piers in 1907–9 to permit grouting of the masonry and underpinning of the whole area of the foundations. The excavations reached 9 ft. (2.74 m) below the old foundations, and in the published description there is no mention of piles. The deepest members of the original construction are described as 'oak cradle foundations ... formed of roughly hewn timbers ... half checked at the cross angles, scarfed at the longitudinal junctions, and pinned together by a number of 1-inch oak pins...' This is clearly a description of branders and the use of the term 'cradle'[27] is unfortunate. It is as old a term as 'brander' but because the form of

Fig. 32. West pier and arches of the Brig of Ayr (1491).

'cradles' has been variable the word has often been applied loosely. When used correctly it has always meant a protective framework *surrounding* a foundation, *not under it*.[28] It was so used in the records concerning the reconstruction of Perth Bridge in 1605–16;[29] of two orders made on the same day one required 'ane new cradill to be sunckin at the south end of the first new foundit pillar', and the other that a new brander should be made for the second pillar.[30] Branders are mentioned several times in these accounts but piles not at all, and the order for the cradle to be 'sunckin' seems to confirm that the timber members of the foundations were laid on the river-bed, not driven into it. Moreover, the omission of piles under this bridge must have been a matter of choice, not necessity, because piling was being used extensively in the bridge at Berwick-on-Tweed at just the same time (1611–25).

Berwick Bridge[31] exemplifies a method which was practised from the medieval period to the beginning of the eighteenth century for bridges in tidal rivers, namely that of building on 'starlings'. Starlings were a prominent feature of some of the oldest and most important bridges in England, including London, Rochester and

Newcastle-upon-Tyne;[32] but all those bridges have gone and the starlings (fig. 31) of Berwick Bridge are probably the best examples now extant. A starling (fig. 33) is an artificial island; its outer skin is a vertical wall of timber piles driven side by side till their heads are only just above low-water level. When the wall was complete some tying timbers were fixed across the top and rubble (which was often

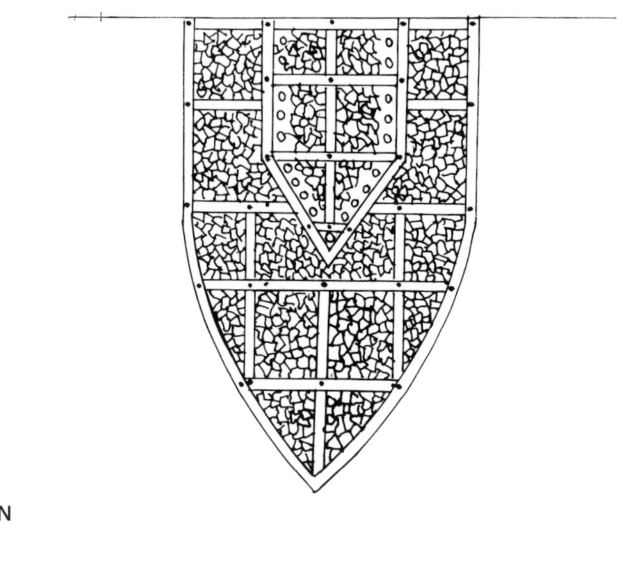

HALF PLAN

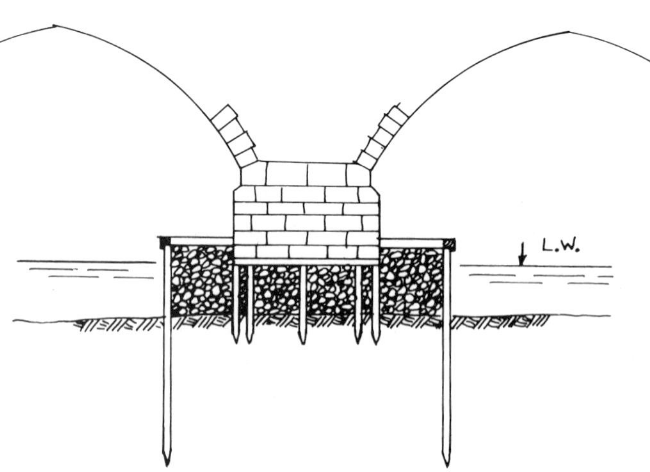

SECTION

Fig. 33. Typical pier and starling.

broken chalk where it was available) was dumped inside until the space was filled up to low-water. The pier could then be built on the top of the starling, working only between tides until the masonry reached high-water level. Further piles were often driven in the area to be covered by the pier, to compact the rubble and give extra support. There was no need for a cofferdam or for artificial lowering of the water level at any stage of the work. In the medieval bridges of many short arches, the starlings obstructed a large proportion of the width of every arch and greatly hindered both the flow of the river and the passage of boats, but at Berwick the arches are larger and the obstruction is not serious.

The starlings have been very well maintained and their top surfaces now are formed of large squared stones contained by well-jointed frames of timber (fig. 31). As already mentioned, most of the money for Berwick Bridge came from the Crown, and the result is a structure that seems to have been more robust, as it was certainly more spacious, than any Scottish bridge built before 1700.

If starlings and hundreds of piles were necessary at Berwick and other English tidal bridges, how were the branders and lowest courses of masonry placed at Bridge of Dee, the Brig of Ayr and the seventeenth century Perth bridge? To these may be added Guard Bridge and the old Dumfries Bridge, which are of similar age and also lack starlings, although they may have piles underneath their piers. Ordinary tides no longer reach the Dumfries bridge as the water level has been raised by a weir some distance downstream, but it was probably in tidal water when first built.

The explanation probably lies in differences of tidal rise between the sites of the English and the Scottish bridges (see Table 2) (p. 88). Unfortunately tide levels are not measured officially at the bridges (except London Bridge) but at harbours somewhere downstream;[33] but there appears to have been navigation through the old Newcastle Bridge at all stages of the tide, and so the level there would not differ from the level at the quays. At Berwick the harbour is very near the bridge and with no obvious difference of water level between them at low tide. In contrast, it is known that at Ayr, Dumfries, Aberdeen, Perth and Guard Bridge the water level at low tide is higher at the bridge than at the adjacent harbour.[34] The height of tidal rise at the bridge is therefore in each case less than that shown in Table 2, but how much less is not known at present. However, when John Smeaton designed his bridge at Perth in 1764 the tidal rise was known to be only 8 ft. (2.44 m) at springs and a negligible height at neaps; he therefore founded the piers inside simple sheet-pile cofferdams protruding about 6 ft. (1.83 m) out of the river-bed, and had no difficulty in pumping them dry—although he had at least considered the idea of stopping work and allowing the tide to fill and flow over the cofferdams for a few days at the springs.[35] His branders were formed on top of driven piles and his lowest courses of masonry laid entirely 'in the dry'. In the absence of other evidence, it must be supposed that the foundations of the older Scottish tidal bridges were laid by similar expedients, but baling, rather than pumping, the water out of the cofferdams and possibly constructing the dams themselves of earthen banks rather than walls of piles. The distinct difference observed in English practice between the methods employed in tidal and in non-tidal rivers is rendered unnecessary if sites are chosen sufficiently far up river to restrict the maximum tidal rise to about 8 ft. (2.44 m). The actual distance up river, however, may differ from a few hundred yards, as at Ayr, to many miles, as at Perth, depending on the gradient of the river-bed and the tidal rise at the mouth. Measurements of tidal rise at the surviving bridges might help to confirm that the Scottish masons' success in building without starlings was due to careful choice of up-river sites.

It is interesting to speculate that the original siting of the towns of Ayr, Perth and Dumfries may have been influenced by the limiting tidal conditions in which it was possible to found a bridge in a medieval cofferdam.

Rubble arches

The masonry of all the oldest bridges now standing is hewn stone in regular courses (see fig. 28). In contrast, rubble was the commonest material all through the eighteenth century. It continued into the nineteenth century, with two important changes: in nineteenth century bridges the joints between archstones are at right-angles to the curve of the arch (i.e. in line with the radius), even when the stones are irregularly shaped, and the wingwalls at the ends of the bridge show a batter, while in eighteenth century bridges the wingwalls have no batter and the joints between archstones can usually be seen to lie above or below the line of the radius over at

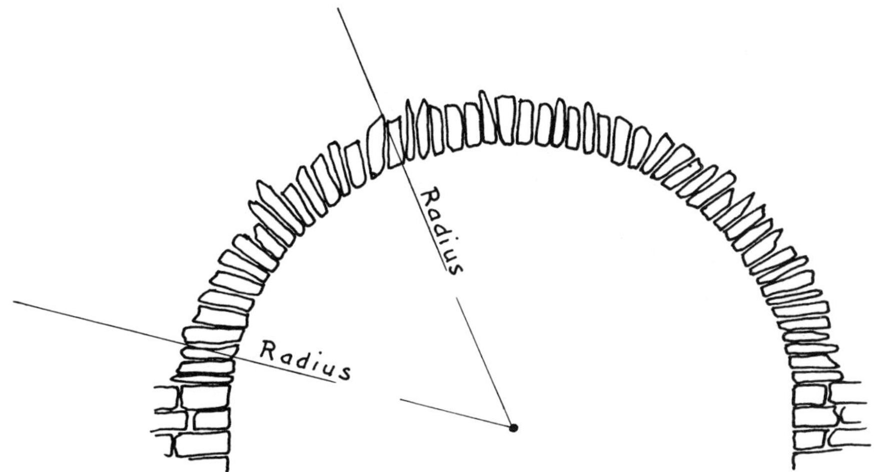

Fig. 34. Typical whinstone rubble arch with irregular angles of voussoirs.

least one or two short lengths of the arch. The sketch in fig. 34 illustrates a typical eighteenth century arch, but the location on the arch of the sections with non-radial joints varies from one bridge to another. Probable methods of construction can be inferred from the pattern of irregular joints in a particular arch.[36] Almost all the bridges which have survived from the first phase of military building in 1725–36 exhibit non-radial arch joints, Tummel and Garvamore Bridges being well-known examples. The arch stones at that time were almost all long, relatively thin, schistose stones of quite irregular shape.

That rubble-arch bridges of this type were built by non-military builders before 1725 is not in doubt, but very few surviving rubble arches are known to have been built before 1700; and this fact provides one strand of evidence that the road from Doune to Kilmahog became the 'carte road' described in the military surveyor's notes (quoted above) at a date before 1700. For convenience the bridges in Table 1 which have rubble arches have been marked (R).

One bridge with an arch very similar to those of the post-1725 military bridges is the old bridge at Carrbridge (fig. 35), and its date of construction is clearly stated in contemporary documents as 1717.[37] There are also a few other bridges in the Highlands which have similar arches but which are not on military routes and may

Fig. 35. Arch of the old bridge at Carrbridge (1717).

therefore pre-date the military work; an obvious example is the old bridge at Invermoriston. In the south, the old bridge at Innerleithen is of fairly similar rubble and was built in 1701.[38] Most of these bridges are of typical 'collection bridge' widths, $6\frac{1}{2}$–$8\frac{1}{2}$ ft. (1.98–2.59 m) between the parapets. At Doune the old Ardoch Bridge, which carried the road eastward to Dunblane, was built 'upon the public expense of the shire' in 1735,[39] almost all of rubble—that is, wingwalls, spandrels and interior of the arch—but with well-squared voussoirs on the faces of the arch and their joints strictly radial. It is $11\frac{1}{2}$ ft. (3.51 m) wide between the parapets. It indicates that the county justices were improving the route out of Doune towards Dunblane at that time. The more important route from Stirling entered Doune from the south over the Bridge of Teith (which had been built in 1535)[40] and could then proceed west towards Callander or Kilmahog on the north side of the Teith. The two bridges on this stretch of road, over Burn o' Cambus about a mile from Doune and over Keltie Water one mile before Callander, are quite different from the Ardoch bridge. Both have spandrels and wingwalls of good rubble but arches entirely of hewn stone in thin courses; the only feature of either arch which corresponds at all with the rubble arches of the military bridges is a slight irregularity in the angles of the arch joints of Keltie Water bridge. The width of each bridge is about $8\frac{1}{2}$ ft. (2.59 m) between the parapets. Their similarity argues that they were built at much the same date and as part of the initial construction (or else a general improvement) of the cart road from Doune to Kilmahog. Their smaller width and their hewn-stone arches suggest that this took place some years before the construction of the Ardoch bridge (1735), but their rubble spandrels suggest that the interval was not too long. A road of some kind from Doune to Callander is marked on Moll's map of Scotland in 1714.[41] Adair's local map,[42] which was probably made between 1680 and 1690, suggests traffic routes by marking bridges and fords rather than roads, but it shows no bridges or fords between Doune and Kilmahog. Bridge of Teith is shown without a road from it to Stirling; there cannot be any doubt that the route was already used, but whether for carts or only horses remains in doubt. Greene's map of 1689[43] shows the towns of Stirling, Dunblane, Doune and Callander, but the only road linking any of them is from Stirling to Dunblane.

From these strands of evidence, the date of construction of a cart road from Doune to Kilmahog, including the two stone bridges, can be placed between 1689 and 1714, and probably before 1700. It appears to be a deliberate, if short, extension of the vehicle road network, and if Inglis was right in his assertion that 'the general introduction of wheeled carriage traffic' took place 'about 1680–1700',[44] it should be possible to find evidence of other extensions of the network in the same years.

The oldest bridge with rubble arches which I have identified is the old bridge at Stow (fig. 36), built for access to the church in 1654–5.[45] It is only $6\frac{1}{2}$ ft. (1.98 m) wide between parapets, and some of the joints between the long, thin arch stones lie as much askew to the radius as in typical eighteenth century bridges. The absence of older rubble bridges may be due to their having decayed more rapidly or to prejudice in earlier years against building with rubble. The major bridges built to the order of bishops in the pre-Reformation period certainly display a high standard of masonry, and it is not unlikely that all but a few of the small and remote bridges were made of timber.

Fig. 36. One arch of the old bridge at Stow (1655).

Table 1

WIDTHS AND DATES OF BRIDGES

A. Bridges carrying important roads at entry to large towns.

Date of construction (completion)	*Grid reference*	*Bridge*	*Width between parapets in feet (and metres)*	*Written source for date*
1409	NN 782010	Dunblane	10 (3.05)	Barty, *Dunblane* (1944)
1415?	NS 797946	Stirling	13 (3.96)	Inglis, *PSAS* 47
1464	NX 968761	Dumfries	14 (4.27)	Edgar, *History of Dumfries* (1746)
1470	NT 251403	Peebles	8 (2.44)	Inglis, *PSAS* 47
1491	NS 338222	Ayr	12 (3.66)	Inglis, *PSAS* 47
1527	NJ 929035	Bridge of Dee, Aberdeen	14½ (4.42)	Fraser, *Bridge of Dee* (1913)
c. 1530?	NT 341725	Musselburgh	11½ (3.50)	Inglis, *PSAS* 47 Graham, *PSAS* 96
c. 1530?	NT 519737	Nungate, Haddington	11 (3.35)	Inglis, *PSAS* 47

Table 1 (*continued*)

Date of construction (completion)	*Grid reference*	*Bridge*	*Width between parapets in feet (and metres)*	*Written source for date*
1607?	NJ 942096	Balgownie, Aberdeen	11 (3.35)	RCAMS, MS notes
1625	NT 996527	Berwick	17 (5.18)	Council minutes, etc.
1684	?	Dumbarton (design)	14 (4.27)	SRO, Register House Plan 3493
1699	NS 868439	Kirkfieldbank, Lanark	13½ (4.11)	Reid, *PSAS* 47
1724	?	Melrose (design)	14 (4.27)	MS estimate (courtesy of R.A. Paxton)
1771	NO 122238	Perth	22 (6.71)	Commissioners' minutes
1772	NS 587647	Broomielaw, Glasgow	30 (9.14)	MS contract

B. Bridges *not* carrying important roads at entry to large towns.

Date of construction (completion)	*Grid reference*	*Bridge (R) denotes arches of rubble masonry*	*Width between parapets*	*Written source for date*
1490?	NS 711578	Bothwell	11½ (3.50)	Inglis, *PSAS* 47
15th century?	NO 133185	Bridge of Earn	12½ (3.81)	Inglis, *PSAS* 47
15th century?	NT 336666	Maiden, Dalkeith	12 (3.66)	RCAMS, *Mid and West Lothian* (1929)
1516	NS 807905	Bannockburn	9½ (2.90)	Inscription on bridge
Early 16th century?	NT 533745	Abbey, Haddington	13½ (4.11)	RCAMS, *East Lothian* (1924)
Early 16th century?	NT 442690	Pencaitland	10½ (3.20)	RCAMS, *East Lothian* (1924); Inglis, *PSAS* 49
Early 16th century?	NS 733546	Avon, Hamilton	7½ (2.29)	Inglis, *PSAS* 49
1530s	NO 452189	Guard	12½ (3.81)	RCAMS, *Fife & Kinross* (1933); Inglis, *PSAS* 47
1530s?	NO 415161	Dairsie	11½ (3.50)	RCAMS, *Fife & Kinross* (1933)
1535	NN 722013	Teith, Doune	10 (3.05)	Inscription on bridge
1539	NO 652662	North Water	12 (3.66)	Inglis, *PSAS* 47
1550	NT 593772	East Linton	8½ (2.59)	RCAMS, *East Lothian* (1924); Graham, *PSAS* 96
Mid-16th century	NS 846952	Tullibody	10½ (3.20)	RCAMS, *Fife & Kinross* (1933)

Table 1 (*continued*)

Date of construction (completion)	*Grid reference*	*Bridge (R) denotes arches of rubble masonry*	*Width between parapets*	*Written source for date*
16th century	NT 652205	Jedburgh	9½ (2.90)	Inglis, *PSAS* 49; RCAMS, *Roxburghshire* (1956)
1619	NT 179755	Cramond	13½ (4.11)	Inscription on bridge
1641	NT 770492	Fogo	8 (2.44)	Inscription on bridge
1649	NS 869443	Mousemill	9 (2.74)	Reid, *PSAS* 47
17th century	NO 400115	Ceres	6 (1.83)	RCAMS, *Fife & Kinross* (1933)
1655	NT 458444	Stow (R)	6½ (1.98)	RCAMS, *Mid & West Lothian* (1929)
1690	NN 706030	Burn o' Cambus	8½ (2.59)	This account
1690	NN 648068	Keltie Water	8 (2.44)	This account
1701	NT 334372	Innerleithen (R)	6½ (1.98)	RCAMS, *Peebles* (1967)
1702	NT 231394	Old Manor (R)	9½ (2.90)	Inscription on bridge
1717	NH 906229	Carrbridge (R)	7½ (2.29)	Contract etc. in Seafield paper, SRO, GD248
1726	NS 896865	Abbeytown, Airth	11 (3.35)	Inscription on bridge
1730	NN 763592	Tummel (R)	12 (3.66)	Contract, SRO, GD1/53/97
1735	NN 730014	Ardoch, Doune (R)	11½ (3.50)	Inscription on bridge
1741	NN 571336	Lochay (R)	12 (3.66)	Inscription on bridge
1745	NS 770956	Drip (R)	11½ (3.50)	RCAMS, *Stirling* 2 (1963)
1764	NN 6658	Kinloch Rannoch (R)	13½ (4.11)	Inscription on bridge

Table 2

HEIGHT OF RISE OF SPRING TIDES
(from *Reed's Nautical Almanack 1980*)

England		*Scotland*	
Berwick	15.4 ft.	Aberdeen	14.1 ft.
London Bridge	23.3	Anstruther (nearest record to Guard Bridge)	19.3
Newcastle-upon-Tyne	17.4	Ayr	9.8
		Perth	11.1

References

1. See above, pp. 49–66.

2. Haldane, A.R.B., *The drove roads of Scotland* (1952), gives a detailed history of individual drove routes from the early sixteenth century.

3. Several instances are quoted by Moir, D.G., 'The roads of Scotland: statute labour roads', *Scottish Geographical Magazine*, **73** (1957), 101–110 and 167–75.

4. Listed in the bibliography of Taylor, W., *The military roads in Scotland* (1976).

5. In the 'Wade Collection' of maps and plans at the Royal Scottish Geographical Society, Edinburgh.

6. *Ibid.*

7. Taylor, *Military roads*, 70–75.

8. Summarised by Salmond, J.B., *Wade in Scotland* (2nd edn., 1938), 120–156, and by Taylor, 46—63.

9. Inglis, H.R.G., 'Ancient bridges in Scotland, and their relation to the Roman and medieval bridges in Europe', *PSAS*, **46** (1911–12), 151–177; 'The roads and bridges in the early history of Scotland', *PSAS*, **47** (1912–13), 303–333; and 'The most ancient bridges in Britain', *PSAS*, **49** (1914–15), 256–274.

10. *PSAS*, **46**, 160–2.

11. *Ibid.*, 162–74.

12. For instance, East Linton bridge has 1762 and 1763 incised on the keystones of arches which are found on careful examination to have been added to widen the original structure.

13. See especially *PSAS*, **47**, 304–10 and **49**, 270–3.

14. *PSAS*, **46**, 164–9; *PSAS*, **47**, 309–15.

15. See *PSAS*, **46**, 171–2.

16. For the construction of Berwick Bridge, see Summerson, Sir John, 'Berwick-on-Tweed Bridge', in Colvin, H.M. (ed.), *History of the King's works*, **4,** part 2 (1982), 769–78.

17. 'Book of bridges belonging to the West Riding, 1752' contains manuscript drawings of all 115. A statistical summary of the facts is given by Ruddock, T., *Arch bridges and their builders, 1735–1835* (1979), 26–7 and 205–7.

18. For the Bridge of Dee scheme see Fraser, G.M., *The Bridge of Dee* (1913), 93–4, and *Reports of the late John Smeaton* (1812), **3**, 51 and pl. 3. For Glasgow Bridge see Renwick, R. (ed.), *Extracts from the records of the burgh of Glasgow*, 7, 418–555 *passim* and Mylne, R.S., *Master Masons to the Crown of Scotland* (1892), 270–3.

19. A summary translation of the accounts is printed *in extenso* in Mylne, *Master Masons*, 18–29.

20. Several continental descriptions of cofferdams survive from the Renaissance period and later; Ramelli, A., *Le diverse et artificiose machine* (Paris, 1588, reprinted 1970), 172–4, gives two illustrations of timber dams with men baling, of which fig. 29 is one.

21. *Master Masons*, 25.

22. Decisions against the use of cofferdams at Westminster (1737–8), Blackfriars (London, 1760) and Bristol (1760–3) are described by Ruddock, *Arch bridges*, *passim*.

23. *Ibid.*, 131. A few engineers refused to believe that man-driven or horse-driven pumps were so limited, notably George Semple and John Smeaton; see *ibid.*, 38–44 and 72 respectively.

24. Letter to James Abernethy, C.E., printed in Mylne, *Master Masons*, 37–8. Fig. 30 is abstracted from the accompanying plate.

25. Unfortunately G.L. Pride, in his very useful *Glossary of Scottish building terms* (1975), gives a meaning which is not sustained by manuscript records of foundation work. His description of 'an iron grille or framework ... as protection at a bridge pier to prevent damage by heavy river-borne articles' is quite incompatible with, for example, the proposal of a 'brander ... laid upon [the bottom of an excavation] ... having two courses of stones ... laid over' for a bridge at Edinburgh through which no water would flow (Ruddock, 'The building of North Bridge, Edinburgh, 1763–75', *Transactions of the Newcomen Society*, **47** (1974–6), 9–33).

26. The whole description comes from Morris, J.A., *The brig of Ayr* (7th edn., 1912), 63–80. Morris was personally responsible for recording the old structure and foundations.

27. Pride's *Glossary* gives 'protective framework' but without specific reference to foundations or bridge piers.

28. The meaning is very clear in eighteenth-century French writing. Gautier, H., *Traité des ponts* (Paris, 1714), 143, gives the following definition: 'On appelle crêche de pourtour, celle qui environne toute une pile, et qui est faite en manière de bâtardeau, avec un fil de pieux, à six pieds de distance ou environ ... pour empêcher que l'eau dégravoye et déchausse sous les fondations.' Note that 'pile' is French for 'pier' and 'pieux' is French for 'piles'.

29. Printed *in extenso* in Mylne, *Master Masons*, 89–97.

30. *Ibid.*, 92.

31. See note 16.

32. See Ruddock, *Arch bridges*, 54–9, for description of these bridges and prints showing starlings.

33. See *Reed's Nautical Almanack 1980*.

34. For information in the hands of the relevant local authorities, I have to thank the Director of Roads, Grampian Regional Council (*per* Mr W. Reid), the Divisional Engineer of Strathclyde Regional Council (*per* Mr S.

W. McFarlane) and the Roads Engineer of Fife Regional Council (*per* Mr W.B. Nield).

35. *Reports of the late John Smeaton* (London, 1812), **1**, 176–7.

36. Ruddock, *Arch bridges*, 21–3, describes military bridges of this type, with three photographs.

37. S.R.O., Seafield papers, GD 248/22/5 (1–3).

38. RCAMS, *Peebles* (1967), **2**, 340–1, no. 628 and pl. 139E.

39. Inscription on parapet.

40. Inscription on parapet.

41. Herman Moll, *The northern part of Great Britain* (London, 1714).

42. National Library of Scotland, 'A map of the countries about Stirling, author Jo Adair'.

43. *A new map of Scotland with the roads by Rob Greene*, n.d. but generally considered to have been published in 1689.

44. *PSAS*, **46**, 164.

45. RCAMS, *Mid and West Lothian* (1929), 175, no. 252 and fig. 25.

Old Bridge, Bridge of Earn, Perthshire: a Posthumous Account

Geoffrey Hay and Geoffrey Stell

The old bridge over the River Earn was one of the large multiple span stone arched bridges of medieval Scotland. The demolition of its last surviving arches in 1976 also gave it the unenviable distinction of being the most important casualty of its kind in recent years. Furthermore, a survey of the remains of the bridge prior to its demolition revealed evidence of an eventful and instructive building history, and this detailed case-study complements Ted Ruddock's general review of the subject. It is based on a rescue-recording operation carried out by the writers for the National Monuments Record of Scotland in 1970. By that time the unsafe condition of the redundant structure had long been giving much cause for concern.[1]

The bridge stood in tidal water at what was presumably considered to be the lowest practicable crossing-point of the River Earn (N.G.R., NO 132185), a few miles upstream from its confluence with the River Tay. At the bridging-point the river follows a general eastward course through a reversed S-shaped meander. On the north bank the approach to the bridge skirts the grounds of Moncrieffe House, a modern reconstruction of the 1679 mansion that was largely destroyed by fire in 1957.[2] The village of Bridge of Earn, whose name obviously commemorates the importance of the crossing, grew up around the southern approach to the old bridge, but the layout and building development in the village shifted westwards following completion in 1822 of a new bridge with a level carriageway some 180 m upstream (NO 131186).[3] This later bridge subsequently served as part of the A90 trunk route but the whole village is now bypassed altogether by the M90 motorway which carries traffic across the River Earn a short distance downstream of the site of the old bridge.

At the date of survey the visible remains of the old bridge consisted of two portions, one on each side of the river separated by a distance of over 59 m (fig. 37). The northern portion, which still

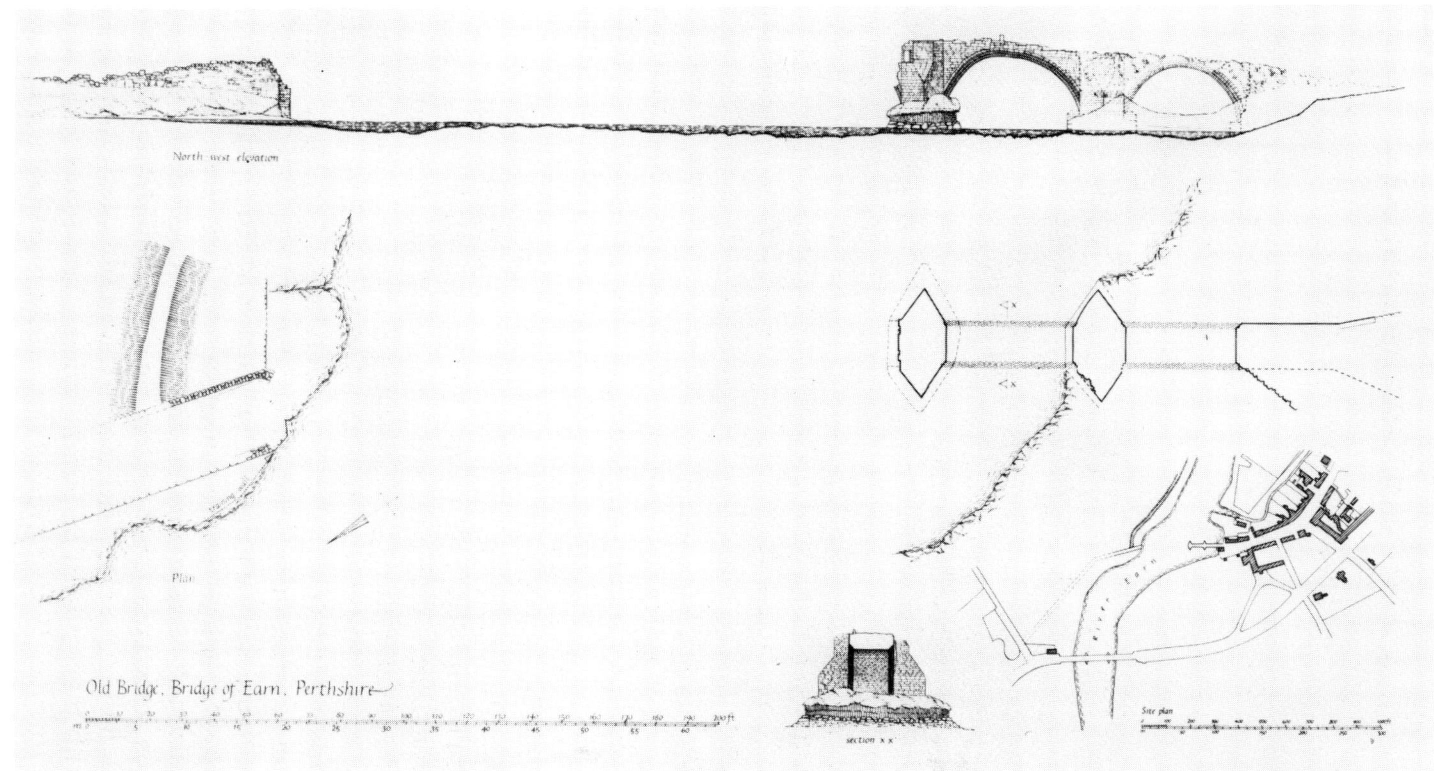

Fig. 37. The Old Bridge, Bridge of Earn: measured survey-drawing of the upstanding remains. Figs. 37–41 are Crown Copyright, RCAMS.

Fig. 38. General view from the north.

survives in much the same condition as it was in 1970, comprises a part of the approach-road, abutment and parapet, flanked by a training-wall to the west and a levée to the east. The remains on the south side comprised two complete arches with their associated landward abutment and piers (fig. 38), all in an advanced state of decay. The southernmost arch spanned part of the flood plain on the south bank. The middle section of the bridge had already been comprehensively dismantled in the nineteenth century, and no traces of it survived above water-level.

The southern approach and the two arches lay in a straight south-west/north-east alignment, a choice of axis that may have been predetermined by the nature of the river-bed. Even from casual observation, however, it was evident that the abutment on the north bank and the angled approach from the north-north-east did not line up with the southern half of the bridge. The 1863 edition of the 1:2,500 Ordnance Survey map,[4] the earliest available large-scale map of the area, showed the north abutment in a position slightly to the east of this projected line, although preliminary sightings made in 1970 demonstrated that it lay to the west. There were also observable differences in the character of the masonry employed at the two surviving ends of the bridge. It was clear from the outset that one of the aims of the survey would be to reconcile these discrepancies between the surviving features on the north and south banks.

Much of the fabric of the bridge as it then survived was constructed of coursed, well-dressed and lime-mortared sandstone rubble masonry. The facework of the spandrels incorporated numerous L-shaped blocks, many of which were interlocked or snecked. The walling of the southernmost arch and abutment was reduced to its rubble core. The masonry throughout showed much evidence of reconstruction and repair, and iron cramps had been introduced in several places. The south and west faces of the north abutment had been reconstructed in ashlar masonry which was characterised by some distinctive diagonal tooling and incised masons' marks. Other masons' marks were also found on the north-east face of the northernmost surviving cutwater. Parts of the bridge that had been demolished in the nineteenth century were known to have been re-used in the enlargement of the nearby private chapel on the Moncrieffe estate.[5]

The two arches were of a slightly distorted semi-circular form, spanning 36 ft. (10.97 m) and 43 ft. (13.11 m) respectively from south to north.[6] The haunch of a third arch on the north-east face of the northernmost cutwater indicated that it too was of semi-circular form with an estimated clear span of about 44 ft. (13.41 m). The intrados of each arch was 11 ft. 6 in. (3.50 m) in width, with a plain soffit of coursed masonry bearing no evidence of ribbed construction. The arch-faces were, however, fashioned with recessed triple ring-members, each wrought with a 4-in. (0.10 m) chamfer and built up in two or three structural orders (fig. 39). It was also observed, although the significance of the detail is unclear, that the outer chamfer was set at a more vertical inclination than the other two. The chamfers died into the springing-points of the arches, except on the western face of the erstwhile third arch where they were corbelled out from the side of the pier. There were no surviving arch-members associated with the abutment on the north bank.

Fig. 39. Detail of springing of southernmost arch.

The two piers were of massive construction. They each had double-sided splayed cutwaters on the upstream and downstream faces, measuring 14 ft. (4.27 m) in width by 34 ft. (10.36 m) in length from tip to tip. The cutwaters were set at right angles to the axis of the bridge, and neither their alignment nor the angle and depth of the upstream-facing splays made any concession to the prevailing south-easterly flow of the river. The base of the north pier was constructed of two courses of vertically-set masonry above a rough boulder-stone foundation-course, achieving a total height of about 8 ft. (2.44 m). The visible substructure of the southernmost cutwater had been refaced in ashlar.

The flanks of the piers were battered, and the tips of the cutwaters had chamfered offsets carried up to form broad refuges. On the north-west face of the northernmost pier there was a carved armorial panel framed within a moulded stone surround (fig. 40). Only the faint, vestigial outlines of the supporters, helm and crest were discernible.[7] At the base of the south-west-facing splay of the same cutwater the date 1761 had been incised, formerly preceded, according to one observer, by the initials IS.[8]

The surface of the carriageway was too disturbed and overgrown to permit detailed investigations, and there were no standing remains of the original parapet-wall. A later reconstructed parapet stood on the east side of the south-western approach; it measured 1 ft. 6 ins. (0.46 m) in width, and the position of a stone fender on the west side of the northernmost arch showed that the parapet had been about 1 ft. 2 ins. (0.36 m) in width at that point. Given an overall width of 14 ft. 10 in. (4.52 m), the carriageway was thus probably between 11 ft. 10 in. (3.60 m) and 12 ft 6 in. (3.81 m) in maximum width; in elevation it rose to a height of approximately 23 ft. (7.01 m) above the base of the piers.

The west flank of the south abutment, which was reduced to its rubble core, represented the remains of a landward cutwater or training-wall. A photograph taken in about 1875 showed this feature in a more complete state of preservation, and at that date its summit-area was occupied by the ruinous gable-wall of a small building, probably a toll-house.[9]

The approach-road on the north bank makes a gradual ascent to the riverside abutment on a vertical-sided walled embankment. The parapets of the flanking retaining-wall have a basal width of 2 ft. 2 in. (0.66 m), reduced to 1 ft. 8 in. (0.51 m) by an internal

Fig. 40. Detail of armorial panel.

scarcement. The carriageway is about 21 ft. 8 in. (0.60 m) wide, but at the abutment the parapets are angled inwards and the width is reduced by a further 7 ft. (2.13 m). Protection for the upstream face has been provided by a low training-wall extending northwestwards from the base of the abutment.

Investigation of the river bed revealed part of a flat masonry platform, the straight north side of which lay parallel to and about 50 ft. (15.24 m) south of the abutment on the north bank. These were evidently remains of a midstream pier and cutwater, whose position and alignment showed that the angled approach from the north had continued in the same line over the northernmost arch. No other foundations were located, but it seemed likely that the change of direction in the carriageway probably occurred at the point where a simple geometrical projection of the two approaches would suggest, that is, just to the south-west of these riverine foundations and well within the possible limits of a broad pier (fig. 41).

The old bridge in its final form was the subject of a lithographed sketch by D.O. Hill in 1821 (fig. 42), the year prior to the completion of its replacement.[10] Although misleading in some minor details, such as the incorrect positioning of the armorial panel, this attractive illustration does provide a useful starting-point for a historical enquiry since it clearly shows the general differences in character between the northernmost arch and the rest of the bridge. The chamfered orders of voussoirs of the four south arches are absent from the plain north arch, while the counterfort of the pier (and the corresponding pedestrian refuge above) is of a broader and more rectilinear shape.

An account of Dunbarney parish written in 1842 confirms what the archaeological and pictorial evidence hinted at, namely, that the fifth arch at the north end was an addition, having been inserted some eighty years prior to that account.[11] From Perth Burgh Records we learn that construction of the additional arch was authorised by the burgh magistrates in July 1765 and that both John Adam, architect, and John Smeaton, engineer, acted as consultants. The actual building works got under way after December 1766 and were supervised by William Watson, overseer of Public Works.[12] The problem that had led to this major undertaking was the continued erosion of the north bank where the river was gradually shifting its course and exerting pressure on the

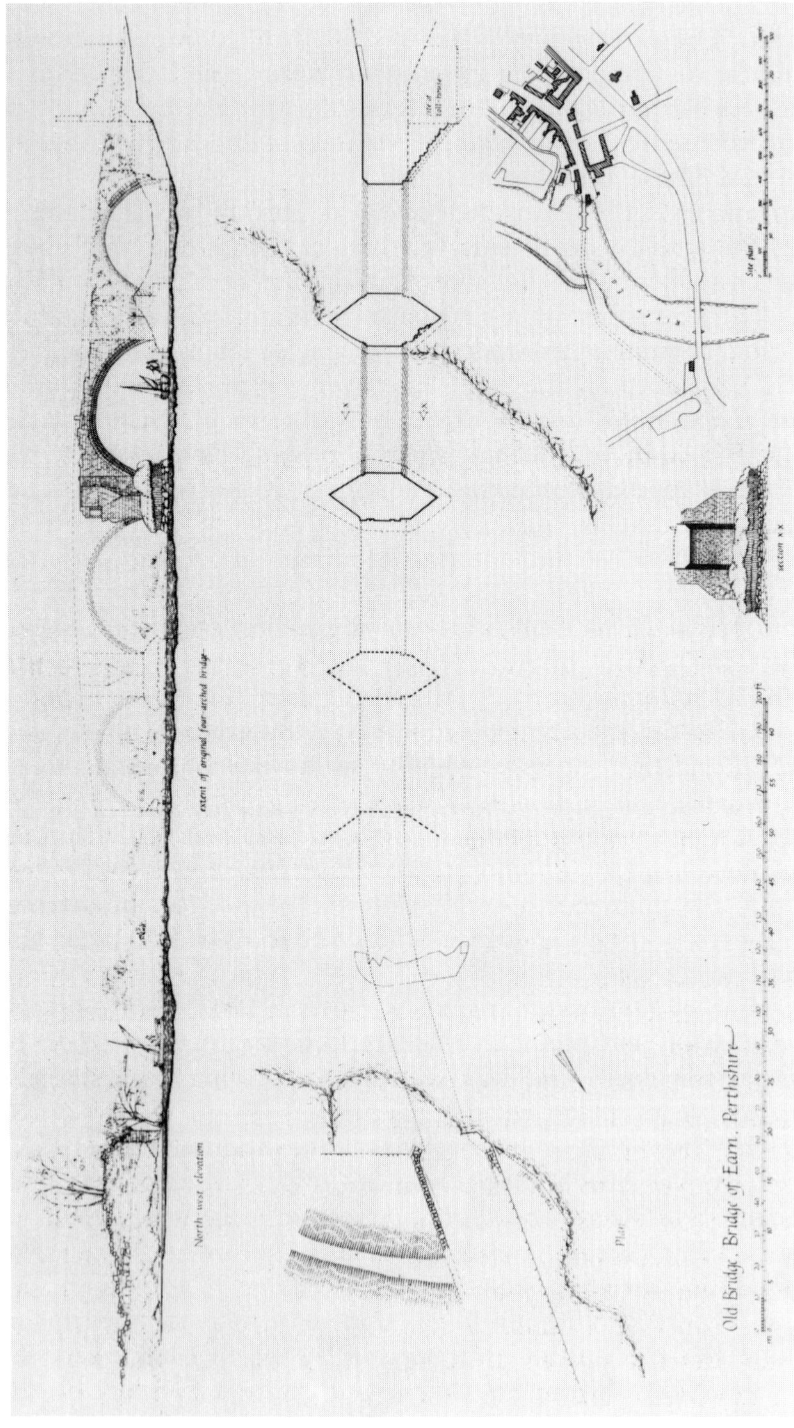

Fig. 41. Measured survey-drawing with suggested reconstruction of original and later works.

Fig. 42. D.O. Hill lithograph, 1821 (from *Sketches of Scenery in Perthshire*).

abutment of the original four-arched structure. The turf-covered eyot that fronts the northernmost pier in Hill's sketch may in fact be a portion of the original river bank. If so, its position provides a dramatic visual measure of the extent of the erosion problem prior to the construction of the additional arch.

Reconstruction and repairs are an inevitable consequence of the structural stresses to which all bridges are subjected. The Old Bridge of Earn was no exception, and, as we have seen, even its last fragmentary stump showed much evidence of necessary maintenance. Most of the repairs and modifications can probably be ascribed to the seventeenth and eighteenth centuries, but only those portions that clearly corresponded to the 1765–66 programme of works, and possibly also the repairs to one of the cutwaters commemorated by the 1761 inscription, can be dated within more precise limits. Its building history was, however, more calamitous than most. An unfortunate choice of site conspired with the effects of poor construction to produce structural problems that required rather more than routine maintenance. The bridge was declared ruinous in 1592, and on 22 January 1614 it was reported that 'the northernmost pend and bow of the Bridge of Erne fell down, being evil bigged from the beginning, filled only with clay and earth, and without any blind pend, as the Brig of Tay has been in the same manner formerly bigged of old. The burgh [Perth] and shire, with all diligence caused David Jack and David Mill, put up the same with timber-work'.[13]

Just how old the bridge was at the date of this collapse is difficult to say. The historical sources, scanty as they are, would suggest that a bridge over the Earn had been built either wholly or partly of stone as early as the second quarter of the fourteenth century. The bridges of Perth and Earn were two of the principal objects for which King Robert I requested the liberty of stone quarrying from local quarries belonging to Scone Abbey in 1326.[14] A payment towards this bridge was entered in the royal Exchequer Rolls in 1329, and, although an entry in the following year referred to the upkeep of a ferry-boat, a bridge over the Earn acquired some strategic military importance in the prelude to the battle of Dupplin Moor in 1332. Either completed or in course of construction, the bridge at that date was evidently guarded by mounted troops and men-at-arms under the command of the Earl of Mar.[15] Payments towards the fabric and other references to a bridge were made in 1402, 1409 and 1530, but the incident of 1614 and the description of it in 1629 as 'four bowes long' provide the first unequivocal correspondence between the documentary and the structural evidence.[16]

Diagnostic features such as the chamfered voussoirs, the size and form of the arches and piers, and the width of the carriageway undoubtedly point to a medieval origin. Some of its characteristics are strikingly similar to those of the four-arched bridge over the Forth at Stirling which has been ascribed to the late fifteenth or early sixteenth centuries.[17] The known or estimated spans of the Earn bridge were smaller throughout, but the side and central spans were of similar relative proportions. Details such as the chamfered double ring-members and the plain soffits of the arches at Stirling are also closely comparable. On the other hand, the sequence from timber to all-stone construction that is reasonably well authenticated at Stirling is not known to have taken place at the Earn crossing. But, given the strong similarities between these two structures in all other respects, it would be difficult to believe that the four-arched section of the Old Bridge of Earn was any older than its counterpart at Stirling; it would be equally difficult to disbelieve that they were of roughly the same age.

References

1. A report by Dr Thomas Ross on the history, condition and possible repair of the bridge in 1910 was published in Moncrieff, F. and Moncreiffe, W., *The Moncreiffs and the Moncreiffes* (1929), **2,** Appendix, 652–8 (typescript MS in the National Monuments Record of Scotland). See also NLS, MS 701, nos. 43–69 for other material on this subject by the same author.

The survey report, drawings and photographs on which this account is based are lodged in the National Monuments Record of Scotland, and this material is used here by courtesy of the Commissioners.

A preservation schedule was placed upon the dilapidated remains in 1940, SRO MW1/1181 (1940), SC 24662/2A Part III.

2. *Moncreiffs, op. cit., passim*; Dunbar, J.G., *Sir William Bruce, 1630–1710* (Scottish Arts Council Exhibition catalogue, 1970), 14.

3. For the replacement bridge see, e.g., *PSAS,* **33** (1898–99), 417 (papers in Perth City Archives); NLS, Rennie Correspondence MS 5111, Box 1, Fl; SRO, Moncreiffe of Moncreiffe Muniments, Box 2, Bundles 13 (5) and 34 (3).

4. 1:2,500 Ordnance Survey Sheet CX, 2, Dunbarney parish, Perthshire, 1863.

5. MacGibbon, D. and Ross, T., *The Ecclesiastical Architecture of Scotland* (1896–7), **3,** 521–2.

6. Cf. figures cited by Inglis in *PSAS,* **47** (1912–13), 310.

7. The arms of the Moncreiffe family, illustrated in *Moncreiffs*, vol. 1, facing p. 126, are carved in relief on one of the panels on the walls on Moncreiffe Chapel. For other armorial panels associated with medieval bridges cf., e.g., RCAMS, *Inventory of Fife,* nos. 178, 389, 405, 417, 470 and 591.

8. Thomas Ross in *Moncreiffs*, vol. 2, 657.

9. Perth Art Gallery and Museum, Magnus Jackson Collection no. 2163 (copy in National Monuments Record of Scotland).

10. Hill, D.O., *Sketches of Scenery in Perthshire* (1821), and see also *D.O. Hill and R. Adamson* (Scottish Arts Council Exhibition Catalogue, 1970), 22, no.7.

11. *NSA (New Statistical Account)*, **10,** 'Perthshire', 811–12 and note.

12. Perth Burgh Records, vol. 1/1/1, an additional new arch to be provided at the North end, 1 July 1765; vol. 1/1/2, the comments of John Adam, architect, concerning the securing of the bridge, 14 August and 2 December 1765; and ibid., John Smeaton's opinions on the proper manner of building to be communicated to Adam, 1 December 1766.

13. *NSA*, *op. cit.*, 821n. 'Blind pend' is possibly drainage-culvert or flood-arch.

14. *Scone Liber,* no. 143.
15. *Exch. Rolls,* **1** (1264–1359), 210, 277; Nicholson, R. *Edward III and the Scots,* 85 and chronicle references cited. Cf. *PSAS,* **47,** 325–6.
16. *PSAS,* **47,** 307, and refs. cited; *Hist. MSS Comm.,* 13th Report, Appendix 7 (Earl of Lonsdale MSS), 87, cited in *Moncreiffs,* **1,** 298.
17. RCAMS, *Inventory of Stirlingshire,* **2,** no. 455.

Wheelless Transport in Northern Scotland

Alexander Fenton

It is no secret that forms of transport of pre-industrial types are important pointers to the nature of life and work in the areas of their occurrence. Equally, forms of transport are themselves shaped by their environment and by the needs of those who use them. There is a constant interaction between community, environment, equipment, and sometimes ways of doing things that involve no equipment. It is such interaction that quietly, and without outside interference, leads to cultural change.

Change due to such causes may be appreciable only at a very local level. Some scholars have objections to closely localised studies on the grounds that, though they may serve as a starting point, yet they do not bring out the importance of the object being researched in all aspects of life, nor do they lead to the formulation of laws of development. But a science cannot be built without bricks, without the clay and straw and water that constitute the bricks, without the sun or the fire that dries or burns them. Every piece of evidence has its part to play in building up a science with its rules and theories and general concepts. Detailed local studies, 'point' studies, are the very stuff of its existence, provided they are put into perspective through wider, collaborative activity.

At the moment, forms of transport are included amongst the themes under consideration for the European Ethnological Atlas.[1] The present account looks at an aspect of transport in the recent and more distant past in the north of Scotland, one of the remote edges of Europe, where roads have been few or makeshift for the most part, until recent decades. A matter of relative chronology arises straight away. To look at transport without wheels, through direct field research and through documentary records of the last 200 years, is in fact to look much further back in time, for some of the surviving methods of transport may be very old. It is also likely that the surviving and documented range of methods is a diminished reflection of the earlier range, for an increasing sophistication of the conditions of life, as in recent generations, may well lead to a reduction in the number of socially acceptable ways of moving objects. Comparison with, say, the range of methods of carrying on the human back still to be found in parts of Europe[2] shows immediately that many more possibilities exist than those indicated by the Northern Scottish evidence. It must always be borne in mind that in this industrialised world, the range of possibilities is at least likely to have been reduced even in relict areas of the most conservative character, though a scholar will always wish to have in mind all he can bring together from comparative study and observation, as an aid to assessing the chronology of the differential rates of development of cultural items and assemblages in the localities with which he is concerned.

If survivals are being sought in this country, it is natural to look to the north and west, especially where roads are few or makeshift. In this area, back transport has survived, in part till the present day, and the choice between the human back and horseback may depend on no more than the distance to be travelled. In fact the amount carried by a small pony was not a great deal more than that put on the back of a human being.

Containers for the purpose took several forms. Baskets and creels were made of straw, rushes, docken stalks, heather or willow, as a domestic craft based on the raw resources of the neighbourhood (figs. 43–45). Few tools were required except for a flat needle of wood or bone with an opening in the broader end.

Nothing had to be purchased. The material was gathered at a suitable period, and the making was done as an evening occupation, or on wet days. Outside influence on form was, therefore, minimal, and variety was due partly to the use to which the baskets were put, and partly to the means of transport. For the most part, baskets carried on the human back were similar to those carried on horseback, though the latter went in pairs. Those for carrying by people tended to be more tightly made to avoid spillage; those for horses were more open. There were also minor differences in shape. In Orkney, for example, the bottom of the basket known by the Norse-derived name of *caisie* was made rounder and more cup-shaped than in Shetland.[3] This is not a difference due to function, but a regional characteristic. Such characteristics have been or are being eroded due to the increasingly general use of canes, which can be readily purchased, for basket-making in Orkney and Shetland. However, in the Highlands of Mainland Scotland, as in the Western Islands, willow canes have long been a more common material for basket

Fig. 43. Annie Harper carrying a basket on her back, with the carrying-band, *fettle*, across her chest. Orkney 1894. I.5.29.

making (fig. 44). In some instances willow has been specially planted in the gardens. The almost treeless conditions of Orkney and Shetland precluded the ready use of this material, until the coming of greater prosperity in recent decades led to the purchasing of prepared cane. As a result, there is some erosion of regional characteristics. Furthermore, as the need for such baskets for carrying manure, and peat for fuel, is coming to an end, so do the

Fig. 44. A wickerwork creel, *cliabh*, loaded with peat. Lewis. C3190.

baskets, in their modern forms, begin to be used as ornamental domestic containers. There is, therefore, a change in status, and further change will undoubtedly come as wickerwork containers kept by the fireside to hold fuel, become adapted in shape to suit modern sitting-rooms, probably in imitation of metal containers in use elsewhere.

Changes in appearance, actual or postulated, are also accompanied by changes in carrying techniques. The normal method in Northern

Fig. 45. A large basket, *koš*, carried with a hooked-stick, *nošarka*, across the shoulder. Liptovska Teplička, Slovakia, 1969. A. Fenton, XXI(a).II.53.

Scotland was for the carrying band to go across the chest (figs. 43–44). This contrasts with the Faroe Islands, north-west in the Atlantic Sea, where the baskets were and are carried by a band that goes across the forehead. The fact that the Faroese baskets are usually of wood does not appear to explain such a difference. But the fact is that carrying-bands are simply becoming handles, baskets are beginning to be lifted like buckets, and back-transport is scarcely respectable.

Change and variation can be observed, recorded, and fitted into theoretical concepts. History and the quest for origins and directions of earlier movement must remain a basic element of ethnological studies, however, and in this respect we can profitably examine the harness of pack-horses.

First, a pad was laid on the horse's back. This could be a lamb- or sheepskin, with the wool still on, or more often a mat of plaited grass, straw or rushes, usually backed by cloth. Even a thin, grassy sod could serve the purpose at times, as was usual in Iceland. In the Northern Isles such back covers measured up to 3 ft. (0.91 m) square. Such covers meant, of course, that the saddle itself did not especially require to be padded. Another point is that though North Scotland is the main survival area, this does not at all mean that back covers were used nowhere else. This is shown clearly by the linguistic evidence alone: *flackie* and *flettie* in Shetland, Orkney and Caithness; *forsel* in Orkney; *fosset*, *leaves*, and *sheemach* in North-East Scotland; *brot*, *brotach* and *brottie* from Banffshire down to Perthshire; *cadda* in the Ulster dialects. There are also a good half-dozen Gaelic terms. In other words, the terminology covers at least the main hilly districts north of the Tay.

Over the cover-pad went the wooden pack-saddle, of which two main forms occur, the split-saddle (figs. 46–48) and the crook-saddle (fig. 49), the former being made in two separate halves, and the latter in one fixed piece. Both types have two flat boards whose inner sides lie against the back cover. It is possible to speculate on the origins of the split-saddle. It was known in the late seventeenth century in the Faroe Islands, and the term *klyfsaďul* was recorded in 1345 in Sweden. In Lapland there are pack-saddles, sometimes highly decorated, used on reindeer. These consist of two curved boards like half barrel-staves, one of which passes through a key-hole slot in the top of the other (fig. 48). There are no side-boards, and the late Professor Stigum in Oslo considered that the side-boards of pack-saddles in Iceland, the Faroes, Shetland and Orkney were the result of influence from the riding-saddle. If this is so, the side-boards or horns represent the oldest element of the pack-saddle in Scotland. Like the Lappish saddle, it may have evolved from the use of suitable branches coupled together. According to oral tradition the 'Lappish' type was formerly known in South-West Norway. Conceivably, it spread west from there to Shetland, Orkney, the Faroes and Iceland, the side-boards being added at the

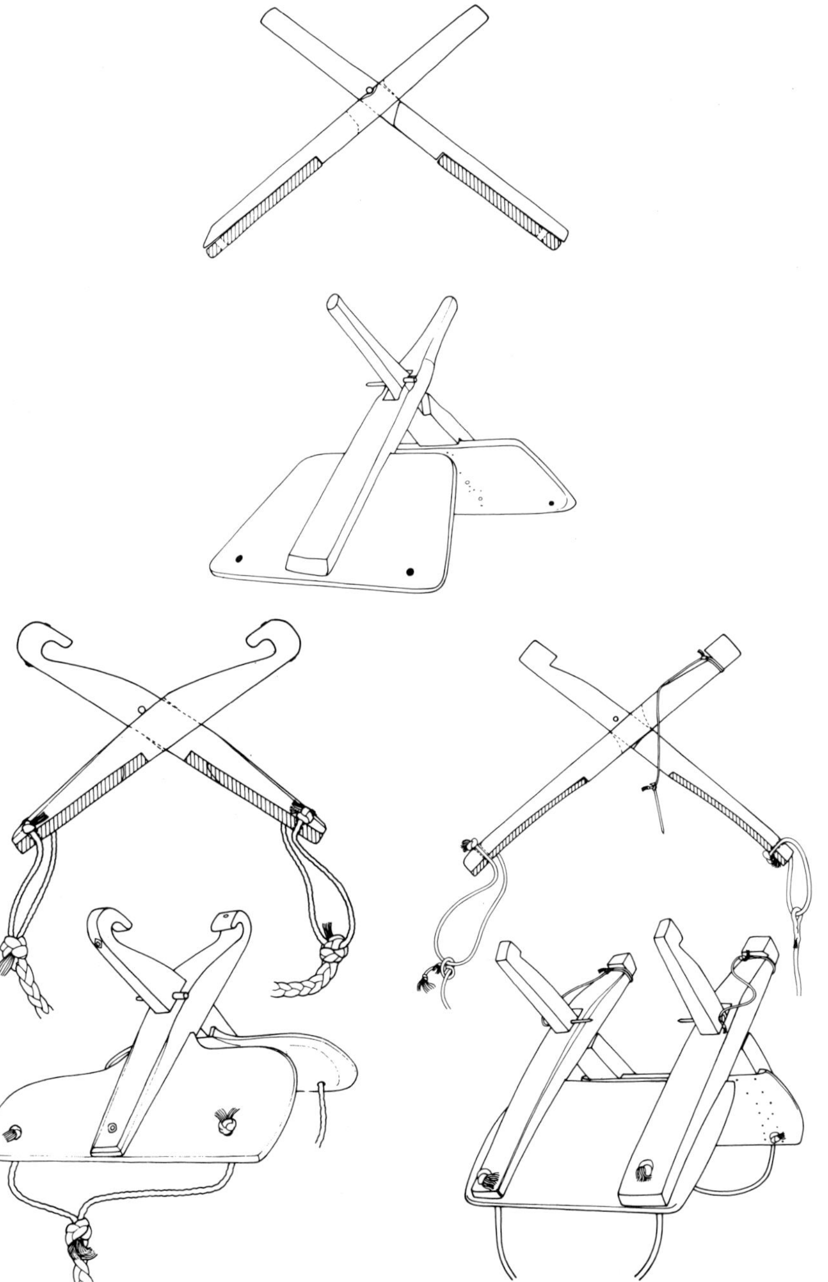

Fig. 46. Split saddles, with one and two pairs of horns: (a) from Papa Stour, Shetland. C226(b); (b) from the Mainland of Shetland. C3187; (c) from Orkney. C226(c).

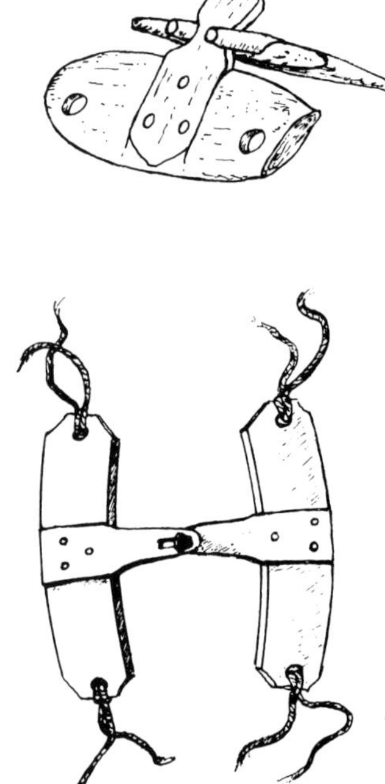

Fig. 47. Faroese split saddles. Top, after Jirlow 1931; bottom, after Svabo, 1781–82. C11403.

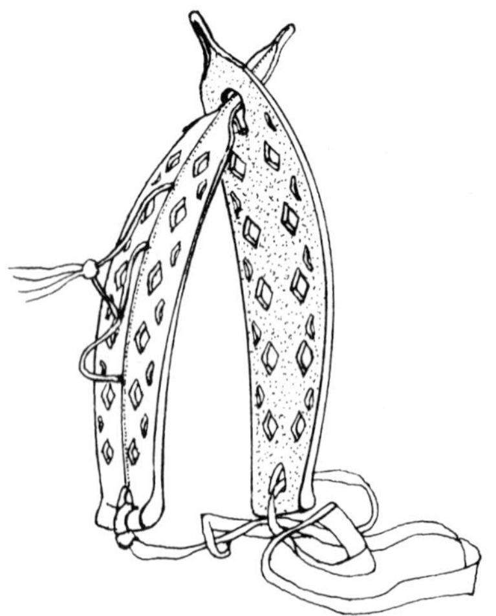

Fig. 48. A Lappish split saddle. After Wiklund, 1938. C11403.

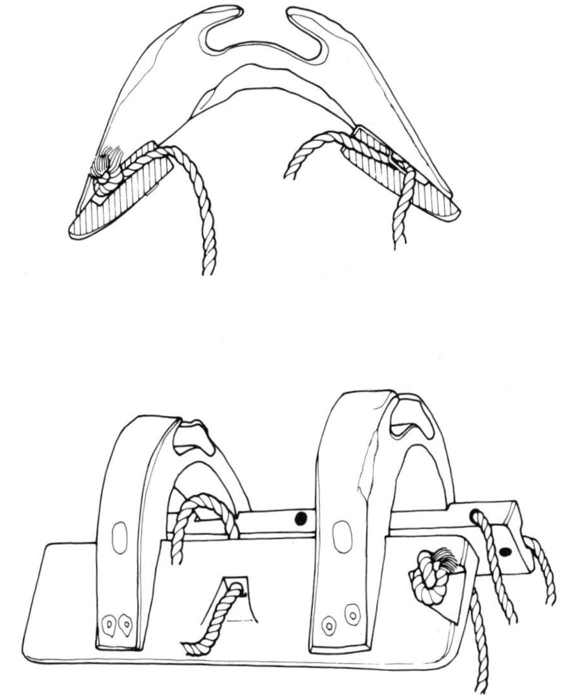

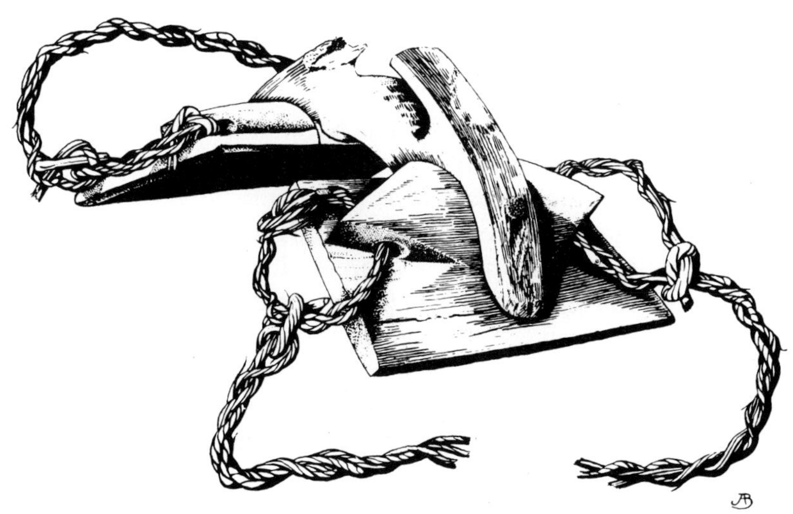

Fig. 49. Crook saddles: (a) from Islay. C226(d); (b) from Rannoch. C3188.

same time or shortly after. Bronze mountings from finds of riding-saddles of the second half of the fifth century A.D. in South Sweden include long, narrow pieces that must have been attached to side-boards at the bottom and then run up the wooden cantles. Some bronze rings were also found, probably attached to the saddle so that bags or burdens could be slung on them. These riding-saddles with side-boards could also be used for carrying light loads, but there is no definite evidence to suggest a date for the transfer of side-boards to the pack-saddle. It could quite well have happened before the Vikings started raiding and settling in North Scotland. The split-saddle is or was distributed in Britain in Shetland and Orkney and possibly Caithness. The only other evidence is from Clare Island in Ireland.

The one-piece crook-saddle may have one or two bows or crooks, each crook having deep notches in which the burden ropes could lie. Crook-saddles were to be found in the Highlands and Western Islands, and at an earlier period in Lowland Scotland as well. The name itself goes back to the sixteenth century in the North-East, and the form of the crook-saddle may be related to that of the cart-saddle or 'car sadil', recorded in old Scots from 1496. A so-called 'hooked car-saddle' for carrying creels was referred to in the Central Highlands in the 1790s. The implication is that the crook-saddle probably spread into the Highland area from the Lowlands, and is therefore unlikely to have the same degree of antiquity as the split-saddle.

Split-saddles are called *clibbers*, or some variant, mainly in the Northern Isles and Caithness; the name 'crook-saddle' was fairly widespread in North-East and North Scotland. Linguistically therefore, as well as on grounds of form, split- and crook-saddles can be separated as belonging to different geographical areas, and having different forms and sources of origin. Scandinavian and Scottish Mainland traditions relating to pre-industrial transport forms, therefore, meet and mingle in Northern Scotland.

The harness ropes were of a variety of materials: straw, rushes, horse hair, twisted birch or willow twigs (fig. 49b), the fibrous roots of the sea-reed, *Arundo arenaria*, seal-skins, and in recent times also twisted silk stockings. The tail girth in the Northern Isles was padded at the back to prevent abrasion, but elsewhere in the West, including Ireland, a wooden crupper was the norm. The tail girth kept loads from slipping forward. To keep them from slipping sideways, there was a belly-band, and backward motion was prevented by a breast-band. This was a rare feature in the Northern Isles, though common enough in the Gaelic-speaking areas and in the Faroe Islands.

The last element of pack-horse harness to be mentioned is the bridle. This had no bit, but only cheek-pieces of wood, or, rarely, iron, which were linked above the nose and behind the jaw. There was also a central opening at right angles to the terminal openings, through which was passed the cord that went over the horse's head, behind its ears. This form of bridle, known in Scots as the *branks*, could also be used for riding horses, in which case a form of bit could be added, but this was not necessary for a pack-horse, which was invariably led by a short length of rope (fig. 51a–b). Sometimes a simple halter of rope, with no cheek-pieces at all, could be used.

The creels and kishies attached to the sides of the pack-saddles were for the most part similar to those carried on the human back. For carrying certain kinds of loads, such as peat, the baskets were placed inside open-work nets, called *maishies*, which gave extra support. Peat could be carried in a net without the use of any additional containers. The bottoms of dung creels were made to open so that a load of manure could be dropped straight down. There were also wooden panniers (fig. 50) used for loads such as

Fig. 50. A pair of wooden panniers from Aberdeenshire. By courtesy of the Anthropological Museum, University of Aberdeen. C364.

hay, corn, straw, ferns or even stones and other heavy materials. These were the so-called *crubbans* or *curracks*. It was not always necessary to use a pack-saddle and creels or curracks for carrying loads. Bags of corn, meal etc. were simply laid across the horse's back so as to balance across it, and were then fastened with a rope around the belly.

Regarding draught, as opposed to carriage on the back, the simplest form of vehicle is the travois or slide-car, in which loads are carried on a pair of poles whose lower ends trail on the ground behind the draught-animal. Though illustrated in Early Bronze Age rock engravings, the earliest actual find of a pair of travois poles seems to be from the moor at Uchte in Lower Saxony. To them had been tied a bundle of clothes which, along with a fibula, are said to belong to the period 300–150 B.C.[4] No indication of the nature of the draught was found, and it may be that the thongs, of which traces were found on the front ends, went around the shoulders of the dead man who was found nearby. It is worth noticing in this context that bundles could also be carried slung on single poles—the Swedes, for example, used the so-called *dragstång* for carrying water.

The earliest Scottish travois illustrations come from John Slezer's *Theatrum Scotiae*, published in 1693 (fig. 51a–b). The areas represented are Dunblane and Arbroath. In each case there is a ribbed framework built across the poles to take loads of hay etc. Next in time is an illustration of the 1730s.[5] Here the poles are joined by a pair of semi-circular hoops. A Perthshire writer of 1799[6] made an important point: he said that such travois or cars succeeded the currack for back transport, and that they required a road or track of some kind, whereas the currack could be used wherever it was possible for a horse to walk. Information about such travois can be got from Arran, Glencoe in Argyll, Loch Tarf in Inverness-shire, the hilly Grampian districts of Angus, Wester Ross, Dumbarton, Stirling, Strathglass in Kintail (fig. 52) etc. from the late eighteenth down to the twentieth century.[7]

Osgood Mackenzie gives a detailed description of their making in Wester Ross in the nineteenth century. Two birch trees formed the poles, with the ends adzed to a suitable angle for sliding on the ground. Two cross-planks were nailed across, and bored to receive 4 ft. (1.22 m) long hazel rungs to form the front and back. There was a plank floor, and the rungs were joined by a plank at the top to

Fig. 51. Slide cars: (a) at Dunblane, Perthshire. C359; (b) at Arbroath, Angus. C360. After Slezer, 1693.

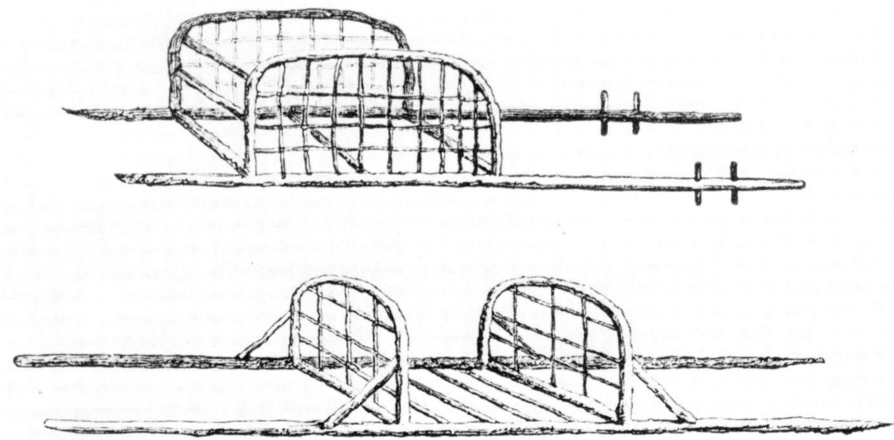

Fig. 52. Slide cars. Strathglass, Kintail, seen in 1863–4. After Mitchell 1880. C587.

give stability.[8] An example seen in Skye in 1867 had a wattle-infilled base; there was also a sturdier version for carrying manure.

In 1863–4 Sir Arthur Mitchell observed two travois in Ross-shire, and he published diagrams of them in 1880. He also set alongside them a copy of the slide-car illustrated by Burt (fig. 53a–b). However, it should be noted that not only has Burt's diagram been turned the other way round, which could have been a printer's error, but a heavy horse has also been substituted for the original pony. If Mitchell was guilty of artistic licence, he nevertheless also made some very percipient remarks, showing that he understood that such apparently primitive transport devices were not a reflection of backward and degraded conditions, but were adapted for work where carts were useless. 'It would certainly show a want of wisdom in the Kintail Highlanders,' he said, 'if they used wheeled carts to do the work they require of their wheelless carts. Indeed, they could not so use these, except by putting the drag on hard and fast—being first at the trouble of getting wheels, and then at the trouble of preventing them turning.'[9]

The travois, then, was commonly used around the Highland fringes. It has survived till the present day in the island of Jura, for transporting shot deer from the hills (fig. 54). This latter-day 'Jura car', however, is a sophisticated joiner-made vehicle. In its simplest

Fig. 53. Slide car: (a) after Burt, *c.* 1734. C3034; (b) the same, after Mitchell 1880.

form of all, it can consist of two poles, pulled by a man, for carrying loads of hay, as I observed in 1969 in Czechoslovakia (fig. 55). If a heavy load such as dung was being moved, a wickerwork creel could be set across the poles of a travois. This was called in North and North-East Scotland a *kellach sledge*. References to it lie broadly within the period 1750–1850 (fig. 56). In Nairn, 1794, it was said to consist of a 'conical basket framed on twigs', supported between the shafts and two linking cross-bars of the travois.[10] Dung baskets appear to have been wide at the mouth and narrow at the bottom, in section like an equilateral triangle, laid on their side on the travois.

Fig. 54. A slide car carrying a shot deer. Finchairn, Argyll. C10103. By courtesy of the Museum of Argyll Farming Life, Auchindrain.

Fig. 55. A 'slide car' made of two poles, used for moving hay-stacks on steep slopes. Liptovska Teplička, Slovakia, 1969. A. Fenton, XXI(a).I.72.

Fig. 56. A kellach cart. After Burt, *c.* 1734. C3033.

A peat basket, on the other hand, was square. But where the terrain was too steep or rough, loads continued to be carried on horseback. There was, therefore, a normal adaptation of equipment in relation to terrain, the nature of the loads, and the presence of roads or tracks, which were evidently desirable even for the wheelless travois.

By the end of the eighteenth century, the pattern had become one of survival and even reminiscence in many areas, but remained one of necessity in others, as in the parish of Kiltarlity in Inverness, where in the 1790s there were 361 sledges, alongside 40 'coups or small waggons' and 376 carts (fig. 57).[11] The minister of this parish did a patient counting job. Survival areas of the same period were Kilfinan, Argyll, where the peat, corn and manure cars and sledges had been largely superseded by 58 carts;[12] Calder in Nairn, where the tenants stuck to their old style equipment;[13] and the moorland districts of Killearn, Stirlingshire.[14] In Torthorwald, Dumfries, the so-called 'trail-cars' used about 1750 were no more than remembered by the 1790s,[15] and no doubt the same could be said for much of Lowland Scotland.

I have not considered wheeled vehicles here, but there is only a short step between the travois and the two-wheeled cart. As mentioned earlier, some kind of road was preferred for the travois.

Fig. 57. A rung cart. After Burt, *c.* 1734. C3032.

This factor may have had some influence in encouraging the addition of a pair of small wheels to the ends of the travois poles. They caused less damage to the roads, and at the same time allowed the carriage of at least slightly heavier burdens. The link can be ascertained also on the basis of terminology, for in areas where the *kellach sledge* was used, the cart was the *kellach* or *kellachie cart*. This 'wheeled travois' was recorded in Ross in 1713, and illustrated in the 1730s by Captain Burt.

In conclusion, a number of points may be stressed. Even within the limits of the material presented, it can be seen that the forms of pack-saddles, baskets, travois and their wheeled equivalents, and the associated terminology, put the Scottish material firmly into a European setting. Indications of evolutionary processes, as in the addition of wheels to the travois, can be seen. Detailed study of the evidence has local value in providing an index to the response to terrain and the effects of tradition, and has general value for purposes of comparison and interpretation. Simple transport methods like some of those described may help to suggest something of the functional pattern of life beyond the period of written history. And the evidence, like so much more of the material culture of earlier communities, throws into clear relief the fact that evolution and change are processes that rarely take place and are rarely done with once and for all, but may be subject to repetition and even occasional retrogression, as the human situation and environment dictate.

References

1. The European Ethnological Atlas is organised by an International Commission which co-ordinates the work of helpers in almost every European country. Its aim is to produce atlas sheets and commentary volumes which document and study elements of traditional culture across existing political boundaries. The material relating to Seasonal Bonfires has already been published. The present writer acts as Secretary to the Commission.

2. See Fenton, A., Podolák, J. and Rasmussen, H., edd., *Land Transport in Europe*, 1973. Relevant contributions refer to the following countries: Czechoslovakia (Baran, 57–64), Portugal (Dias, 109–20), the Carpathians (Kopczyńska–Jaworska, 325–46), Bulgaria (Marinov, 356–62), Hungary (Paládi–Kovács, 395–407), the Faroe Islands (Baldwin, 31–41; Rasmussen, 415–22), Scotland (Fenton, 121–71).

3. Fenton, A., *The Northern Isles. Orkney and Shetland* (1978), 248–50.

4. Dieck, A., Eine Stangenschleife der Ripdorfstufe im Kreise Nienburg/Weser. *Nachrichten aus Niedersachsens Urgeschichte* No. 28 (1959).

5. Burt, E., *Letters from a gentleman in the north of Scotland* (1754, reprint 1974), **1**, facing 75.

6. Robertson, J., *General view of the agriculture of the county of Perth* (1799), 92–3.

7. See Fenton, under note 2.

8. Mackenzie, O. H., *A hundred years in the Highlands* (1924), 31–2.

9. Mitchell, A., *The past in the present* (1880), 97–8.

10. Donaldson, J., *General view of the agriculture of the county of Nairn* (1794), 15.

11. *OSA*, **13** (1794), 519.

12. *OSA*, **14** (1795), 239.

13. *OSA*, **4** (1792), 356.

14. Ure, D., *General view of the agriculture of the county of Dumbarton* (1794), 115.

15. *OSA*, **2** (1792), 4.

Sources of Illustrations

Burt, E., *op. cit.*

Jirlow, R. En lapsk klovsadel och dess ursprung, in *Rig* 1931.

Mitchell, A. *The Past in the Present* 1880

Sleezer, J. *Theatrum Scotiae* 1693

Svabo, J.C. *Indberetninger fra en reise i Færøe 1781 og 1782* (ed Djurhuus, NN.) 1959

Wiklund, K.B. Die Renntierzucht, in *Folk-Liv* 1938

The Distribution of Carts and Wagons[1]

Alexander Fenton

Wheeled vehicles have a long history and wide distribution. This in itself makes them a complex subject for study, to which the attention of many writers has been turned for linguistic, technical, historical, ethnic and other reasons. Though much has been written, the differences of approach mean that a consistent body of comparative data does not exist. There are also many areas for which information on wheeled vehicles is scanty or absent.

Both of these points create difficulties in mapping the diffusion of carts and wagons. A standardised means of extracting data from existing sources is required, in order to construct maps that override national boundaries, as the European Ethnological Atlas seeks to do. To simplify the exercise, I deal here only with vehicles used primarily in agriculture, but even so the subject remains complex.

Gösta Berg's pioneering work on *Sledges and Wheeled Vehicles* was published in 1935. Though described on the title page as 'ethnological studies from the viewpoint of Sweden', nevertheless it was and remains amongst the best comparative regional studies that have appeared.

Professor Berg provides a comparative basis on which it is possible to begin thinking about the construction of maps for types and structural elements. Though many detailed regional studies are needed to fill the numerous gaps, nevertheless a considerable amount of fresh material has been published since 1935, particularly within the last fifteen years. Examination of a selection of these serves to highlight some of the problems and complexities of the subject.

For England, J.G. Jenkins, in *The English Farm Wagon* (1961), has surveyed 600 wagons and established the existence of 28 wagon districts on the basis of types. Though questions of evolution are touched on, mainly following the writings of V.G. Childe, J.G.D. Clark, J. Czekanowski, A.G. Haudricourt and G. Berg,[2] the main strength of the book lies in its technical description of the details of wagon construction, and in its analysis of regional varieties.

Jenkins considers that the heavy wagon for the long-distance transport of goods was probably introduced into Britain from the Low Countries in the sixteenth century, though baggage and passenger wagons were known in Britain before then. At first the heavy wagon served primarily for road transport, but with the rapid spread of agricultural improvement in the eighteenth century, it began to be adapted by local cartwrights for agricultural work, especially harvesting, and even replaced two-wheeled carts for this purpose, though not in areas where the ground was hilly or uneven. The two-wheeled cart was retained in Northern England, Ireland, the Isle of Man, and parts of Wales.

However, the situation must not be over-simplified. Even within these regions, there is evidence to suggest that four-wheeled wagons, usually ox-drawn, existed prior to the spread of the heavy wagon in England for agricultural purposes. There were, for example, four-wheeled chariots in Ireland, drawn by horses.[3] On the estates of landed proprietors in Scotland, there were wagons drawn by oxen yoked in pairs to a central draught-pole, used mainly in the south and east, but with outliers as far north as Shetland and Orkney. Wagons of English type, horse-drawn, did reach the south of Scotland in the second half of the eighteenth century, but they were few in number, and their life-span was short.[4] They marked the absolute limit of the northwards diffusion of such vehicles in Britain. On the other hand, the source of origin of the pole-drawn ox-wagons, used on estates for moving heavy loads, and earlier for heavy goods required for military purposes, remains to be established. Their existence does show that the glamour of the English farm wagon should not be allowed to obscure an apparently earlier pattern of a different character and source.

The English farm-wagon itself could have more than one source of origin. Apart from direct introduction from the Low Countries, it could also derive from the two-wheeled cart. According to Jenkins, the deep-bodied, blue-painted East Anglian wagon is descended from the East Anglian tumbril, itself a descendant of the medieval box-cart. The postulated course of development is based partly on the fact that the East Anglian wagon body is markedly box-shaped, and partly because of the custom of temporarily converting two-wheeled dung-carts into wagons by the addition of pairs of fore-wheels and forecarriages. Such 'hermaphrodite' vehicles, 'partaking of both a cart and a wagon', are known from the end of the eighteenth century. They were made from the indigenous tumbril, or from the lighter Scotch or Leith carts that were imported from Scotland into the East of England. If the tumbril was used, the shafts were removed and a coupling pole was fixed from the cart axle to the forecarriage axle. With the Scotch cart, the front ends of the fixed shafts were made to rest on the forecarriage axle,[5] but the two points of contact must have given rise to turning problems. The use of the Scotch cart with fixed shafts, therefore, is likely to have been a fairly temporary expedient.

It could be argued, in general, that the hermaphrodite combination, whether with Scotch cart or tumbril, is later than the wagon, possibly a poor man's version of it. Nevertheless the existence of the central coupling pole in the case of the tumbril relates it to a method of wagon-body construction widely known elsewhere, in which a pole or—in German—*Langbaum* links two carts or the front and rear portions of a wagon (fig. 58). Putschke's analysis of early archaeological sources points to a distribution of such a body structure in Norway and Sweden (rock carvings dated to about 1200 B.C.), Gotland, Jutland, and West Prussia–Pomerania, with a variant type in Bohemia–South Germany, France, Italy and Spain. His more recent sources show the *Langbaum* in South Norway, South Sweden, South Finland, Denmark, Central England, the Netherlands, Belgium, France, Germany (excluding the Rheingebeit), Switzerland, Upper Italy, Czechoslovakia, Poland, the Baltic, Russia, Austria, Hungary, Rumania, Jugoslavia and Bulgaria.[6] The construction was so common in some areas that a writer could say of feudal Poland, that the distinction between the two-wheeled cart and four-wheeled wagon was of relatively little importance in that country.[7]

This feature, therefore, has a wide distribution. It goes far back in time, it has relevance to theories about the evolution of wagons, and it underlies the problems that may arise from defining carts and wagons too closely as different species. It therefore has considerable ethnological significance.

Jenkins' study of the English farm wagon shows that four-wheeled wagons with pairs of shafts for horse draught developed as agricultural vehicles in England mainly in the eighteenth century, with some possible structural cross-fertilisation from the tumbril and to a lesser extent the Scotch cart. The evidence for ox-drawn wagons with central draught poles from Scotland may point to the

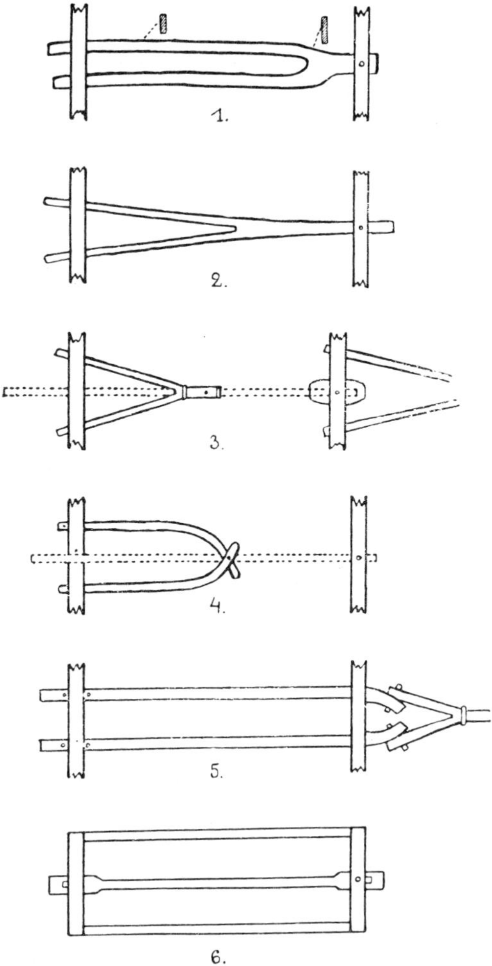

Fig. 58. Methods of linking the front and rear ends of wagon bodies. 1. Carpathians, 2. Polesia, 3. Carpathians, 4. Bulgaria, 5. Bosnia, 6. White Russia. From Moszyński I (1967), 653 (see note 24).

earlier existence of such vehicles in other parts of Britain as well, though it is not possible, for lack of sources, to point to any clear link with either the four-wheeled Irish chariots or the wagons used in England for road transport of loads before the eighteenth century. At any rate, when the horse-drawn wagon became a primary means of farm transport, it led to a considerable, if sometimes only temporary, displacement of two-wheeled carts.

These included the deep, heavy tumbril of the East Anglian plain and the long cart or flat-bodied cart with shafts, sometimes known as a *wain*, and traceable back to the fourteenth century at least. The Scotch cart with its fixed shafts was related in form to the wain, though in Scotland the wain may have originally had a central draught-pole.[8] Etymologically, the word 'wain' is cognate with 'wagon', though the former refers to a two-wheeled and the latter to a four-wheeled vehicle—a fact which further helps to obscure the difference between carts and wagons. The name survives especially for the 'Cornish wain' of South–West England.

In the nineteenth century, circumstances began to change and the use of the wagon began to dwindle. Throughout much of England it was gradually replaced or complemented by the Scotch cart, exported by sea from Leith or by land across the Border into Northern England, and later made in quantity by English firms such as Crosskill of Beverley and Tasker of Andover.[9] The Scotch cart also penetrated Ireland in the late eighteenth-early nineteenth century,[10] as well as the Isle of Man, where it was used alongside the smaller Manx *stiff-cart*, the body of which could be tipped up.[11]

The Scotch cart is a representative of a widespread type. Though it may originally have had a single draught-pole, like the Portuguese carts, in its expansion phase it had a pair of shafts that were extensions of the side-members of the flat body. One horse was enough to pull it, a fact that may have been instrumental in its adoption in Eastern England to replace the two-horse tumbril. On the other hand, its adoption in Ireland and the Isle of Man was related to its greater carrying capacity in relation to existing vehicles.

According to an early nineteenth century writer, it had wheels about 4 ft. (1.2 m) high, and:

> 'differs from common English carts in having scarcely any sides or ends, consequently there is none of the superfluous weight of the tumbrel, and the axle-trees being straighter it runs more truly than common carts; the bottoms of the sides of these carts project like handles behind the cart, to prevent it from falling too far backwards when empty, and to assist the carter in unloading'.

The same writer noted that this type was also common in the Low Countries and in many parts of France, and that in Ireland

> 'the Scotch or Leith cart, as it is called, though it costs full three times as much as a common car, is becoming general in every part of

the country, though it has not been introduced into it more than five or six years'.[12]

Thus, whilst the wagon made considerable progress in the early stages of adoption for farm work, spreading right into parts of Wales[13] and just reaching the south of Scotland, nevertheless it suffered a reversal during the nineteenth century when the Scotch cart pushed it back again. It is evident, therefore, that chronological factors must be kept firmly in mind when mapping carts and wagons in Britain: the distributional patterns for, say, 1700, 1800, and 1900 will be very different. The interpretation of the factors—economic, social, technical, geographical—that give rise to such differences is a matter for regional research, which must eventually be slotted into wider issues, and if this is done cartographically, then selection must again be exercised. In British terms, both the four-wheeled wagon and the flat-bodied Scotch cart with its fixed shafts have relevance to the wider European pattern. The dynamics of their interaction within the national boundaries may help to explain, or provide comparative data for, parallel phenomena in other regions.

For such comparison to be readily carried out, more studies like F. Galhano's on the ox cart in Portugal are required. This, complemented as it was in the year of its publication by a companion volume on the yoking of oxen,[14] is a substantial contribution to the study of the cart. The data are summarised on a distribution map that distinguishes four main cart types, according to the form of the body, suspension, and wheels. Chronological depth is given to the map by the use of red symbols for carts recorded for the period 1960–70, and blue symbols for those of earlier periods.

Galhano pays close attention to the influence of topography in relation to distribution and type. In the flat regions of South Portugal, carts have been at home for centuries. In the hilly parts of North and Central Portugal, carts were fewer in numbers, and mainly restricted in use to the roughly-paved roads. Here, river-transport and sledges were the common alternatives.

In the northern half of the country, the draught animals were exclusively oxen, attached by yokes to the central draught-pole, and the carts had movable axles that turned along with the block wheels, making a loud creaking or groaning noise. In the south, there were carts with spoked wheels that turned on fixed axles, drawn by teams of two or four horses or mules, known from the late eighteenth century. The northern type, therefore, is the older stratum.

To understand and map the Portuguese situation properly, Galhano has in the first instance examined the technical factors—body construction, axle and wheels, and the influence on the cart of the kind of the draught animals. To continue his survey in equivalent depth over the rest of the Iberian peninsula would help to round off the picture that has begun to be painted here.[15]

At the same time, it is of importance to observe the effect on the carts of the use of pairs of yoked oxen. Usually the draught-pole is single, and runs straight back under the cross-planks of the cart floor. In other cases the side supports have been brought forward and curved together to join at the front, forming a single pole to which the centre link of the yoke was attached. This latter form involves skill on the part of the joiners, and was enforced by the use of oxen and the wooden yoke. It would have been much simpler to extend the side supports to make a pair of shafts, as happened in the case of the Scotch cart, which may well have developed out of a wain with a single central draught-pole, after horses replaced oxen as draught animals. Under such circumstances, it may be argued that for international mapping, the important constant feature is the flat body construction and the single pair of wheels, whereas the draught arrangement is dependent on external factors less directly related to the nature of the vehicle.

Of the twenty contributions in the volume *Land Transport in Europe*,[16] seven are concerned with wheeled vehicles, in Scandinavia, Scotland and Wales, Austria, Bulgaria, Czechoslovakia, and Poland. None of these is a detailed study of carts and wagons, but some relevant points may be extracted.

In feudal Poland, a light one-horse cart was in use alongside a two-horse wagon for agricultural work and short-distance transport, and the four-horse wagon for longer-distance and often commercial transport. The one-horse cart could have fixed shafts like the Scotch cart, or the shafts could be separable. In North-East Poland, the shafts were linked by a bow-shaped *duha* above the horse's neck and shoulders from at least the sixteenth century.

Carts with central draught-poles, implying ox draught, are not mentioned for this part of Poland, but they occurred, though rarely, in Czechoslovakia. They had block wheels. Light carts with flat bodies and pairs of shafts were, however, more common. The unimportance of the distinction between two-wheeled carts and four-wheeled wagons is emphasised in relation to the small carts of southern Wallachia in Central Slovakia as being 'in fact, half a four-wheeled waggon, essentially lighter and more convenient for mountainous terrain with steep fields'. In turn, this raises the question of whether the cart evolved from the wagon or the wagon from the cart. This question can only be resolved with reference to local conditions. There may be no generalised answer to it.

In the mountain areas of Bulgaria small carts with draught-poles were in use, and larger carts for carrying meal, grain, etc. complemented wagons elsewhere. Some of the carts had shafts within which the ox or horse walked. Generally speaking, the two-wheeled carts were mostly confined to the hilly regions, and some were similar to the front end of a wagon, except that they had smaller spoked wheels. Elsewhere the wagon was the normal vehicle, with a versatile body that could be lengthened, shortened, or made narrower, depending on the load to be carried. The only major variant feature is the stake-brace linking the outer end of the axle with the upper end of the corner post of the wagon body, as found in North Bulgaria.[17]

Apart from the increasingly elusive differences between carts and wagons, three features may be selected here for examination: the stake-brace (figs. 59–61), which appears to be confined to wagons; the use of shafts as against a central pole; and the *duha*, which is associated with pairs of shafts, whether fixed or movable.

Berg records the distribution of the stake-brace as including, in whole or in part, Albania, Austria, Czechoslovakia, Germany, Hungary, Jugoslavia, Lithuania, Poland, Rumania, Russia and Sweden.[18] Ten years earlier Nopcsa had suggested that the stake-brace was a Slavic feature.[19] Berg's noting of the feature over a much wider area showed that Nopcsa's thesis could not be readily maintained. Furthermore, the name for the stake-brace found in some form or another in numerous Central European languages appears, like the names for a number of other cart and wagon parts, to be German in origin, even though the subsequent wider spread may have been through Hungary and other countries.[20] It can be seen, therefore, that a combination of the precise mapping of the full distribution of a feature such as this, in alliance with a study of the terminology, serves as a valuable corrective to theories based on insufficient evidence, and provides clearer historical perspectives.

Fig. 59. A gypsy wagon with a straight stake-brace linking the outer axle-ends with the frame, in Hungary. The wagon is drawn by a single horse yoked at one side of the pole. A. Fenton, 1971.

The use of pairs of shafts, implying horse-draught, is said to have reached the West with the Germans, who must have got them from the Slavs. They were used on both two- and four-wheeled vehicles.[21] Amongst the Baltic peoples and the East Slavs, with the exception of areas such as Estonia, South-West Finland and North Kurzeme, the horse is usually regarded as the earliest draught animal, hence the early use of shafts. The pendulum kept swinging, however, for though the horse was apparently the earlier work animal amongst the East Slavs, it was later in part replaced by the ox in White Russia and the Ukraine (though not in areas such as the Steppes). In Lithuania the ox appeared alongside the horse in the thirteenth century, and had become general by the fifteenth to sixteenth centuries. Eventually the horse came back into its own, for a bad horse was cheaper than a pair of oxen. The use of equids or bovids, therefore, was likely to effect changes in the incidence of use of pairs of shafts, or of central draught-poles. In the 1920s, for

Fig. 60. A loaded wagon with stake-braces, at Bedenik in Jugoslavia. A. Fenton, 1975.

example, the East Slavs usually used a pole and yoke for oxen, and a pair of shafts with a collar and bow (*Krummholz* or *duha*) for horses; but west of the Dniepr, in South-West Ukraine, a pole was standard for both horses and oxen, and neither collar nor bow were used (except in one or two districts). Here shafts were found mainly on sledges drawn by single horses. There were also areas where the pole was unknown.[22]

Such regional variety is in part a reflection of the earlier historical changes that have taken place in the kind of draught animals employed, and also in relation to changes in harness, such as the adoption of the collar that allowed the horse to oust the ox from heavy ploughing. The bow or *duha*, that appears to go back to the fifteenth century in Russia and the Baltic,[23] helps to hold the shafts apart and acts as a kind of shock-absorber on rough roads. It is regarded as a later improvement in Poland,[24] and it therefore seems to have spread from its kernel area of early horse-draught, but it is unlikely to be as old as the use of pairs of shafts themselves.

Fig. 61. a–b A hay-wagon, *rebriňak*, at Liptovska Teplička, in Slovakia. The wagon beam linking the fore and aft portions can be clearly seen. A. Fenton, 1969.

Though the stake-brace is limited in its distribution, nevertheless it is such a readily recognisable feature, with such a well-defined terminology, that it might well be included in a map of special features of wagons. It has a history of at least 500 years, it remains in use, it can point to historical situations of both a national and international character, and it also has importance from the technical point of view. For example, in North Poland, wagons had stake-braces only with rack-frames, whereas in the south they were used with dung-wagons as well.[25] Such variations have been ascribed to ethnic influences, but it is preferable not to prejudge this issue until the full distribution has been mapped, and regional historical situations annotated.

The second and third features referred to, the shafts and bow or *duha*, clearly relate closely to the kind of the draught-animals. The comments made above, allied to points already made such as the likely pre-eighteenth century existence of central draught-poles on wagons or wains in Scotland, show how complicated this aspect of transport is. The distinctive *duha*, like the stake-brace, could and should be mapped,[26] but the question of paired shafts and central draught-poles depends very much on period, and it would probably be just as relevant to plot the distribution of equids and bovids as draught-animals, as the draught-arrangements for the vehicles themselves. It is not certain that either of these tasks could be done easily for an international atlas, for lack of adequate comparative data, nor that a sufficiently clear picture would emerge, because of the number of possibilities for regional variation and preference in relation to social, economic, geographical and other factors, though the effort would be worth making. The issues are further obscured by small points, like the fact that oxen wearing collars may also be found within a pair of shafts, and in parts of Central Europe a single horse may often be seen pulling an empty or lightly-laden wagon, yoked to the side of a single draught-pole (fig. 59).

If this is accepted, then we can begin to think about what would be of positive immediate value for purposes of international cartography. The simplest matters to deal with are readily identifiable features like the stake-brace. But of more general value would be to establish the distribution of farm-vehicles with two or four wheels, or even three wheels, as in some parts of the Low Countries where the custom developed of adding a third wheel to the fronts of dung-carts, possibly in the late eighteenth–early nineteenth century.[27] Such three-wheeled varieties, however, may be of more local than general significance, and do not affect the main issue, which would be to test the validity of the cart and wagon zones outlined by Professor Berg and subsequently adopted by writers such as J.G. Jenkins.

In his notes on the mapping of European carts and wagons prepared for the European Ethnological Atlas Meeting at Visegrád in Hungary in 1974, Professor Berg stated that he regarded it as of main importance to establish the distribution of three main varieties of farm-vehicle: the Mediterranean cart, drawn by a pair of oxen (occurring sporadically as far north as South-West Finland); the Central European wagon, drawn by a pair of oxen or horses; and the North European wagon, usually drawn by a single horse.

It might be preferable in fact not to apply such specific adjectives as 'Mediterranean', since this could pre-suppose a concept relating to a point of origin, which might later have to be adjusted.

Professor Berg considered that if specific aspects were to be taken further, then the following points might be looked at:

1. For carts, the distribution of block wheels and perhaps of rotating axles.
2. For wagons, the different devices for lengthening and shortening the body.

Since the fixed or adjustable wagon-beam is 'the distinguishing characteristic of European wagons'[28] it deserves particularly close attention. Like the keel of a ship, this beam is the foundation on which the rest of the wagon is constructed, whatever the kind of body fitted. And it is hard to avoid thinking, at the same time, of the central draught-poles of the Portuguese carts described by Galhano, which are carried back in one piece as the main support for the cart body. If such a correlation is valid, it can establish a further formal link between the cart and the wagon. As long ago as 1929, Moszyński constructed a diagram showing a variety of wagon-beam types (fig. 58) which could now be supplemented by incidental information from a variety of sources.[29] Carts as well as wagons could be included in a survey of the structural forms of the bases of wheeled vehicles.

Mechanisation has so overtaken animal-drawn farm-transport in so many areas, that the mapping of carts and wagons has already become in part a historical exercise. Nevertheless such vehicles survive widely still, and where they do not, they nevertheless lie within memory. The time is ripe, therefore, for a general survey based on a select number of the most important and most readily comparable elements.

In the foregoing pages, a number of regional studies were looked at to see what problems and what common features were to be found. Gösta Berg's *Sledges and Wheeled Vehicles* comes closest to being a general survey, and in this respect, there now falls to be examined a much more recent work—Wolfram Putschke, *Sachtypologie der Landfahrzeuge* (1971) based on data published up to about 1966 known to him.[30]

Putschke's technique was to look at the subject widely in time and space so as to examine questions of origin, development and diffusion. However, because the scope of the subject is so vast, and because there are such large gaps in the information available, he had to apply to his study of this aspect of material culture a technique more commonly used by word geographers. The publication is part of a dissertation on *Wort topologische Untersuchungen im Sach- und Nennstrukturat der Landfahrzeuge* (word topological research into the structure and terminology of land transport vehicles), presented at Marburg in 1966. This involved taking an early and a later period, that may be labelled 'archaeological' (prehistoric and early historical) and 'ethnological', and examining the evidence for each period in terms of typology and diffusion. The two periods were then related through the needle's eye of what he called *Sachprojektiv* (object projection). This attempt to use ethnological evidence inferentially to expand and clarify the archaeological evidence is bold and interesting, though it need scarcely be pointed out that the work would have benefited from the existence of a better range of detailed ethnological studies. The archaeological side has been much more intensively studied, as Putschke's wide-ranging survey of the literature shows. It is also no surprise that the complexity of the subject should have brought Putschke to the conclusion that it could not be reduced to monogenetic or polygenetic theories of origin, but was conditioned by a whole set of associations and relationships.[31]

It is evident, in fact, that material culture, which can be affected by so many diverse factors, is less amenable than words or names to the kind of methodological approach used by Putschke, and his effort to reconstruct the course of development between the periods of his two sections does not quite come off. Nevertheless the book includes many valuable pointers to profitable directions for future activity, and provides a useful guide for thinking about the mapping of carts and wagons.

The primary purpose of such mapping, on a European scale, is to establish an accurate, cartographically expressed corpus of factual data which will reveal patterns on the basis of which theories relating to evolution, diffusion, etc. may be reliably based. At some stage complementary maps relating to types of draught animals, and to wheelless forms of transport, will be required to fill out the picture properly, but a start can be made by mapping types and typological features of carts and wagons, with emphasis on the basic elements—wheels and axle, frame and construction, draught equipment and draught animals. The function of the vehicle also has a close relationship to its body structure. Furthermore, it might be wise not to worry too much about differences between carts and wagons in the first instance, for these are not everywhere mutually exclusive as vehicle types.

The distribution maps made by Putschke are interpretive. In pursuing questions of origin, evolution and diffusion, he maps the various aspects of his subject in the light of possible antecedents, and marks likely lines of diffusion with arrows. The maps that are most straightforward and most relevant for our purpose set against each other the archaeological and ethnological evidence for the distribution of wagons with and without wagon-beams, and of two and three-wheeled vehicles with draught poles or shafts. The maps are, essentially, visual reference summaries for the detail of the text, and though they are small, they are nevertheless instructive and coherent enough to show that the mapping of carts and wagons for the European Ethnological Atlas can be a feasible and fruitful proposition.

Published work shows unambiguously that the mapping of animal-drawn carts and wagons used in farm-work is of value for comparative research. With careful selection of the features to be plotted, and attention to the chronological compatibility of the evidence from published or questionnaire sources, a sound basis should be provided for relating the theme and its various features to geographical space, and new patterns and relationships should become evident.

References

1. This account is an adaptation of one by the present writer that appeared in *Ethnologia Europea* IX:1 (1976) 1–13.

2. Berg, G., *Sledges and wheeled vehicles*, Nordiska Museets Handlingar: 4 (1935); Childe, V.G., True or continuous rotary motion, in Singer, C., Holmyard, E.J. and Hall, A.R., edd., *A history of technology* **1** (1954); Clark, J.G.D., *Prehistoric Europe. The economic basis* (1952); Czekanowski, J., Z Dziejów Wozu i Zaprzęgu, in *Lud* (1952); Haudricourt, A.G., Contribution à la géographie et l'ethnologie de la voiture, in *La revue de géographie humaine et d'ethnologie* (1948); Jenkins, J.G. *The English farm wagon* (1961).

3. Joyce, P.W., *Social history of ancient Ireland* (1903).

4. Fenton, A., *Scottish Country Life* (1976), 205–7.

5. Jenkins, *op. cit.*, 120, 122, 179.

6. Putschke, W., *Sachtypologie der Landfahrzeuge. Ein Beitrag zu ihrer Entstehung, Entwicklung und Verbreitung*, Schriften zur Volksforschung: 4 (1971), 74–7. I am indebted to Professor Günter Wiegelmann, Münster, for lending me this thesis.

7. Jewsiewicki, B., Les types de char utilisés en Pologne féodale, in Fenton, A., Podolák, J. and Rasmussen, H., *Land transport in Europe* (1973), 304.

8. Fenton, A., 1976, *op. cit.*, 205–6; *SND (Scottish National Dictionary)*, see under *Wain*.

9. Jenkins, J.G., Two-wheeled carts, in *Gwerin* II/4 (1959), 173–5.

10. Evans, E.E., *Irish folk ways* (1957), 176–80; Herring, I., The Scottish cart in Ireland and its contemporaries, *c.* 1800, in *Ulster Journal of Archaeology* 7 (1944); [Gailey, A.], Some transport survivals, in *Ulster folk life* **21** (1975), 13; Thompson, G.B., *Primitive land transport of Ulster,* Belfast Museum and Art Gallery Transport Handbook No. 2 (1958).

11. Killip, I., Stiff-carts and spinning-wheels, in *Journal of the Manx Museum* **VI**/7 (1960–61), 117–8.

12. Edgeworth, R., *An essay on the construction of roads and carriages* (1813), 100, 103.

13. Peate, I.C., Some aspects of agricultural transport in Wales, in *Archaeologia Cambrensis* (Dec. 1935), 231–2; Jenkins, J.G., Sledges and wheeled vehicles in Wales, in Fenton, Podolák and Rasmussen, *op. cit.,* (1973), 270–93.

14. Galhano, F., *O carro de bois em Portugal,* Centro de estudos de etnologia (1973); Oliveira, E.V.de, Galhano, F. and Pereira, E.B., *Sistemas de atrelagem dos bois em Portugal,* Centro de estudos de etnologia (1973).

15. Cf. Ebeling, W., *Die landwirtschaftliche Geräte im Osten der Provinz Lugo (Spanien)* (1930), 54–94, 143–45.

16. All in Fenton, Podolák and Rasmussen, *op. cit.*: Jewsiewicki (Poland), *op. cit.*, 300–3; Baran, L., Transport in Czechoslovakia as an ethnographical and social phenomenon, 76; Marinov, V., Traditionelle Transportmittel in Bulgarien, 367, 370.

17. Vakarelski, Ch., *Bulgarische Volkskunde*, Grundriss der slavischen Philologie und Kulturgeschichte (1969), 131–33.

18. Berg, *op. cit.*, 165–7.

19. Nopcsa, F., *Albanien. Bauten, Trachten und Geräte Nordalbaniens* (1925), 139.

20. Czekanowski, *op. cit.*, 10–12.

21. *Ibid.*, 4–8.

22. Viires, A., *Über historisch-kulturelle Beziehungen in landwirtschaftlichen Transport der Völker der Ostbaltikums* (1964), 2; Zelenin, D., *Russische (Ostslavische) Volkskunde*, Grundriss der slavischen Philologie und Kulturgeschichte (1927), 130–31.

23. Viires 1964, *op. cit.*, 4.

24. Moszyński, K., *Kultura Ludowa Słowian I* (1929, new edition 1967), 659.

25. Czekanowski, *op. cit.*, 12.

26. Cf. Viires, A., Über die Herkunft und Verbreitung des Krummholzes im Pferdegeschirr, in Szabadfalvi J. and Ujváry, Z., edd., *Studia ethnographica et folkloristica in honorem Béla Gunda* (1971). See also the important new book by A. Viires, *Talurahva Veovahendid. Baltimaade Rahvapärate Pollumajanduslike Veokite Ajalugu* (Farm transport. The history of popular rural transport in the Baltic region) (1980).

27. Theeuwissen, J., *Het landbouwvoertuig in de etnographie van de Kempen* (1969).

28. Berg, *op. cit.*, 158.

29. E.g. Moora, H. and Viires, A., *Abriss der estnischen Volkskunde* (1964), 126 (Estonia); Dunăre, N., *Tara Birsei* (1972), I. 369–71 (Rumania); Fél, E. and Hofer, T., *Geräte der Átányer Bauern* (1974), 424–5 (Hungary).

30. See Putschke, *op. cit.*, 16, for a list of studies that go beyond regional boundaries.

31. *Ibid.*, 98.

Index of Places